Body of Work

PORTFOLIO / PENGUIN

BODY OF WORK

PAMELA SLIM is an author, speaker, and mentor in the new world of work. She spent the first ten years of her solo practice as a consultant to large corporations such as Hewlett-Packard, Charles Schwab, and Cisco Systems, where she worked with thousands of employees, managers, and executives. In 2005 she started the *Escape from Cubicle Nation* blog, which is now one of the top career and business sites on the Web. She has coached thousands of budding entrepreneurs in businesses ranging from martial art studios to software start-ups. Her first book, *Escape from Cubicle Nation*, won best small-business book of 2009 from 800-CEO-Read. Pam lives with her husband and two kids in Mesa, Arizona, where she fends off suburban attackers at the grocery store with her black belt in mixed martial arts.

Body of Work

*Finding the Thread That Ties
Your Story Together*

PAMELA SLIM

PORTFOLIO / PENGUIN

PORTFOLIO / PENGUIN

Published by the Penguin Group
Penguin Group (USA) LLC
375 Hudson Street
New York, New York 10014

USA | Canada | UK | Ireland | Australia | New Zealand | India | South Africa | China
penguin.com
A Penguin Random House Company

First published by Portfolio / Penguin, a member of Penguin Group (USA) LLC, 2013

LIBRARY OF CONGRESS CATALOGING-IN-PUBLICATION DATA
Slim, Pamela.
Body of work : finding the thread that ties your story together / Pamela Slim.
pages cm
Summary: "These days it's increasingly rare to have a stable career in any field. More and more
of us are blending big company jobs, startup gigs, freelance work, and volunteer side projects.
We take chances to expand our knowledge, capabilities, and experience. But how do we make
sense of that kind of career-and explain it? Pamela Slim, the acclaimed author of Escape from
Cubicle Nation, gives us the tools to have meaningful careers in this new world of work. She
shows how to find the connections among diverse accomplishments, sell your story, and
continually reinvent and relaunch your brand"— Provided by publisher.
ISBN 978-1-59184-619-2 (pbk.)
1. Career development. 2. Job satisfaction. 3. Success in business. 4. Job skills. 5. Expertise.
I. Title.
HF5381.S6219 2014
650.1—dc23
2013037302

Printed in the United States of America
1 3 5 7 9 10 8 6 4 2

Set in Adobe Caslon Pro
Designed by Spring Hoteling

For Darryl, Josh, Rosie, Jeffery, and Cecy,
for making our home a place of continual grace, love,
laughter, and creativity. All that I do is for you, and because of you.

And for my mom, who has taught me that cultivating a happy,
healthy, secure family is a work of art, and a revolutionary act.

CONTENTS

Contents

Body of Work

CHAPTER 1

Your Body of Work

Life isn't about finding yourself. Life is about creating
yourself.

—George Bernard Shaw

The white paint was peeling, and chunks of plaster were
missing from the exterior walls. Most of the windows were
broken. Rusted swings hung from an iron frame, and the
tattered playground sat on twisted pieces of asphalt. Graffiti
and trash littered the outside of the building.

For two decades, members of the small California coastal
town of Port Costa, population 200, had walked and driven
past the old fading schoolhouse without giving it a second
thought. The town was a mix of antiques shops, aging homes,
and old shipyard buildings, so a bit of decay did not seem out
of the ordinary.

But my dad saw something else.

Under the cracked paint and broken windows, he saw a vibrant, rich community center.

"The first time I saw the Port Costa School, I knew it was made to be an institution of learning. It was supposed to be filled with people learning Spanish, or painting, or tap dancing," my dad said.

The building had not been used as a school since 1966. And so despite having no plan, no experience with historic-building restoration, no construction skills, and no way to raise the hundreds of thousands of dollars required to fix the school, my dad and Diane, my bonus mom (my term for stepmom), decided they would purchase the building.

The fact that my dad would take on such an audacious challenge was not a surprise to me. All my life, I had watched him embrace the craft of his photography, obsessing over the perfect shot. When I was in preschool, I attended city council meetings in San Anselmo, California, where for three years, he patiently worked to establish the state's first curbside recycling program, in 1971.

After decades of observing my dad work, I realized that he was not just building a career (although he was a very successful professional photographer), he was not just being a volunteer (although he spent hundreds of hours of unpaid time on community projects), but he was creating a deep and rich **body of work** that not only had great meaning and significance to him but also created considerable change and value in his community. It didn't really matter if a project was overwhelming, or even impossible; if it fit with his vision of what he wanted to create for himself and for the world, he embraced it. It was an inspiring lesson for me.

As I watched the global economy fall to pieces in 2007 and sink into deep recession for a solid six years after that, creating fear and stress and uncertainty in workers of all stripes, it dawned on me:

My dad just might hold the secret to thriving in the new world of work.

How do you make sense of your career in a work environment that no longer has any predictable career paths?

How do you create stability in a world that has no job security, uncertain markets, threats of terrorism, and a fiercely competitive global workforce?

How do you balance making a living with making time for family, health, and recreation?

How do you develop relationships with mentors when everyone is so busy?

How do you keep your skills relevant in a world that moves so quickly that companies are launched, or destroyed, in a day?

How do you plan for your financial future when you have no idea if your income stream will slow to a trickle, or even dry up completely if you get laid off or go through a difficult stage of business?

Standard career advice would say to get more education, work harder, and make yourself indispensable to your organization or customer base.

This advice made a lot of sense in the twentieth century. In the twenty-first century, this advice is incomplete.

I have spent the last twenty years coaching thousands of employees, executives, and entrepreneurs in a huge variety of industries. I have watched organizations start, grow, shrink, and implode. I have sat across the table from longtime employees and watched them get laid off. I have helped start hundreds of new companies.

From these experiences I know the following to be true:

No one is looking out for your career anymore. You must find meaning, locate opportunities, sell yourself, and plan for failure, calamity, and unexpected disasters. You must develop a set of skills that makes you able to earn an income in as many ways as possible.

The new world of work requires a new lens and skill set to ensure career success. You must create your own body of work as you toil in different organizational systems and structures.

When you view your career through the lens of an overarching body of work, you:

- know the deeper roots that connect your entire work and life experience.
- count all significant experiences and skills in your life as "ingredients" that can be put together into interesting new "work recipes."
- are not afraid of pursuing work inside and outside of companies.
- base career decisions on your ability to foster skill development and meaningful creative output, as well as financial stability.
- choose to work for organizations that share your values and interests.
- contribute significant, useful, and beautiful things to the world.

- are aware of the risks and pitfalls in the creative process and have the tools and resources to deal with them.
- have mental clarity, intellectual rigor, and self-awareness.
- have an active, motivated, and engaged group of peers and mentors.
- live by a very personal definition of success.
- can tell a clear, compelling story about your work path at each stage of your career.

In my dad's case, he was a professional photographer and journalist. He worked most of his career for Pacific Gas and Electric Company (PG&E), detouring for eight years to work for an oil company before returning to PG&E and staying until retirement.

He survived multiple layoffs through the decades—the most noteworthy when ten of the eleven staff members in his department were laid off, leaving him shell-shocked and alone in his office.

In such a volatile environment, he did some specific things:

- He always focused on the mastery of his craft, inside and outside of work.
- He never got lazy, or took his work for granted. Although I never heard of a situation where a client was unhappy with his photographs, he still worried every time he sent in a job.
- When he got divorced, he took a manual labor job

at an oil company. He hated it with a passion. But he kept plugging away so he could provide for himself and his kids, did freelance photography on the side, and waited for the opportunity to go back to PG&E. It took eight years.

- He showed deep respect for everyone he came in contact with, especially the frontline employees who were repairing power lines in the middle of a storm. He never forgot what it was like to do manual labor and related to them with humility and compassion.

- He truly appreciated his role inside a large organization that provided financial stability as well as many opportunities to grow professionally.

- He was passionate about community service. He was one of a handful of volunteers who recycled all the glass and aluminum in Port Costa every two weeks for thirteen years.

- He showed his kids and grandkids how enriching work can be when one truly delights in its craft. We were all inspired to pursue meaningful and significant careers.

My dad turned sixty-five in November 1999, making him eligible for retirement benefits. In December 1999, he was laid off with a severance package. To this day, at the age of seventy-eight, he still does freelance projects for PG&E.

Was my dad lucky? Very. But I think the fact that he always viewed his career as more than a straight and narrow path, and always as a more cumulative and connected body of work, saved him from layoffs, opened up new opportunities, and allowed him to feel great success and satisfaction in his life.

What exactly is a body of work?

As Daniel Pink wrote in *Drive*, "The secret to high performance and satisfaction—at work, at school, and at home—is the deeply human need to direct our own lives, to learn and create new things, and to do better by ourselves and our world."

Your body of work is everything you create, contribute, affect, and impact. For individuals, it is the personal legacy you leave at the end of your life, including all the tangible and intangible things you have created. Individuals who structure their careers around autonomy, mastery, and purpose will have a powerful body of work.

For organizations, it is the products, property, inventions, ideas, and value they share throughout the course of their existence. Organizations that structure their internal strategies around autonomy, mastery, and purpose will be more competitive and resilient.

Smiling and waving at your neighbor every morning as you get the paper can contribute to your bigger desire to see more civility and joy in the world.

My passion for and commitment to individual determination and transformation has led me from community development projects on the outskirts of Bogotá, Colombia, to science and art education to teaching martial arts to corporate consulting to parenting to blogging to entrepreneur coaching and writing books. And it will take me in new directions in the future, without having to feel constrained by any one audience or business or job title.

A body of work is big and deep and complex. It allows you to experiment and play and change and test.

It supports creative freedom.

It includes obvious things, like books, software code, photographs, videos, process improvements, paintings, and stories.

And not-so-obvious things, like community development, love, movements, memories, and relationships.

Bodies of work often have big overarching themes, such as:

Solving complex problems—like David Batstone's commitment to end human trafficking with his nonprofit advocacy organization, Not For Sale.

Building bridges—like Kai Dupé and his work to bridge the digital divide in technology for people of color.

Changing the world through powerful communication—like Nancy Duarte, who has changed the way business leaders create and deliver presentations.

Making the world more accessible to more people—like Glenda Watson Hyatt, the Canadian writer and motivational speaker with cerebral palsy who writes with her left thumb.

Strengthening the bond between parents and children—like Marilyn Scott-Waters, a children's book author who has created a world of free paper toys at thetoymaker.com.

Each of these examples shows a deep commitment to a cause or problem that is bigger than any one job title or profession or business. And they can include a whole range of output, including writing, physical products, legal legislation, systems, speeches, books, conversations, and advocacy.

Focusing on building a body of work will give you more freedom and clarity to choose different work options throughout the course of your life, and you'll be able to connect your diverse accomplishments, sell your story, and continually reinvent and relaunch your brand.

You won't have to say things like "I am throwing away ten years of studying and practicing law if I start a yoga studio."

(Don't worry—your relatives will say it.)

Or "I am undermining my potential if I take a job as a barista" after you get laid off from your corporate job as a highly paid creative.

If your body of work is about creating beauty and art, why not make lovely images in latte foam while you retool for a new job?

It's also possible to contribute to your body of work if you work in a cubicle inside a larger company.

While the organization may have amnesia about your contribution to its body of work, you know what you created and what you are capable of.

If you completed a huge, significant project, did a spectacular job, and it ended up getting shelved right before being launched, you still did all that work. It may not become part of the organization's legacy, but it is part of yours.

That's why they call it work

Much of today's business literature is focused on short-term gains, hacks, tweaks, and quick wins.

Everyone wants the secret formula. Or the four-hour workweek. Or the easy life on the beach.

Viewing your life as a body of work is not a short-term game.

You want to focus on meaning, skill development, professional network development, craft and mastery. There is no one right answer for everyone.

When my neighbor across the street decided to enroll in an MBA program, she was concerned that her employer would feel it was distracting from her day job. So she didn't tell them.

The mother of two small children, she left the house at 7:00 A.M., worked all day, got home to feed dinner to her kids, put them to bed at 8:00 P.M., then worked again until midnight. Then she got up at 4:00 A.M. and worked some more.

On weekends, her husband took the kids to the zoo or the aquarium or the park—or all three—while she did her homework.

There were many times when I would meet my neighbor in the middle of the street after both of us pulled into our driveways. I saw dark circles under her eyes and heard the strain in her voice. The fatigue in this kind of situation is so deep that you wonder if you will ever get out of it.

My neighbor graduated with a 4.0 GPA. And *then* she told her employer what she had been doing for the last two years. They were stunned that she was able to handle such outside responsibility and still do a great job at work.

My neighbor, her husband, and their kids sacrificed a

lot so she could add marketable skills to her list of ingredients.

Was it a struggle? Absolutely. Was it worth it? Absolutely.

In the big picture, it is worth it to gain skills and experience that open up better opportunities and industries. She is now positioned to be much more competitive in the job market. And with her broad business skills, she may consult from home so she can spend more time with her kids.

It is not all about you

Focusing on your entire body of work rather than solely on a you-centric career has the additional benefit of helping you peer out from behind the curtain of anonymity.

I often run into clients who get anxiety thinking about what could happen if they gain exposure and notoriety.

What if I don't have all the answers?

What if my life is not all together?

What if I have spinach in my teeth when I'm interviewed by Matt Lauer?

When you realize that your job is to contribute to your broader body of work, you can conjure up the following visualization:

Imagine you are standing up on a big stage with a large space in front of you. This space represents your body of work—the thing you care most about creating.

Now visualize many people staring directly at you in the form of big beams of light right at your head.

Now strap a mirror to your forehead.

Take all these beams of light and direct them from your head to the body of work in front of you.

Notice how the more people who are staring directly at you, the more illuminated and bright your body of work is?

Fame is fleeting.

Consistent impact over the course of your life on a body of work you care about deeply is *legacy*.

How do you build a body of work?

There are very specific skills and steps involved in creating a body of work.

These steps are as relevant to a recent college graduate as they are to a senior executive looking for a new challenge.

You will go through these steps at multiple points in your lifetime. They will change depending on your interests, needs, and life situation. For some people, goals will be set for the next one to three years. For others, for five to ten years. You should choose the time frame that works for you. Use the following steps to shape your body of work. Throughout the book, you'll explore each step in more detail, with stories, case studies, tools, and personal reflections.

1. Define your root: Which ideas drive you emotionally? Whom do you want to help? What specific changes do you want to create in the world?

2. Name your ingredients: What are your skills, strengths, and ideas? Which life experiences make you unique, talented, and capable?

3. Choose your work mode: Think about the positions you've had in the past and how you work best. For this next stage of your career, do you want to be an employee, entrepreneur, or freelancer?

4. Create and innovate: What do you want to bring to life at this stage of your career?

5. Surf the fear: Define, understand, and manage your fears and anxieties. They are a key part of any endeavor.

6. Form your team: Gather a specific group of peers, mentors, and collaborators to help you reach your goals.

7. Define what success means to you: Identify specific, relevant, and meaningful financial and personal goals.

8. Sell your story: Tie it all together to create a compelling story to convince potential employers, clients, or partners why you are the perfect person for the mission.

Ready to get started?

Exercise: Body of Work

Imagine yourself many years in the future, on the last day of your life, looking back at the things that you created, developed, nurtured, and contributed. What, ideally, would you like to see?

What do you want to create?
- Write—books, blog posts, e-books, code
- Program—classes, events, workshops, software

- Change the world—movements, organizations, awareness, insight, permission
- Be an artist—art, pictures, music, poetry

Who do you want to help?

- What are the specific characteristics of people you want to work with?
- Why do they deserve the very best of your intelligence and energy?
- What will they do with what you give them?
- Will they appreciate your gifts and bring out your best self?
- Are they fun and engaging to work with?
- Do they push you to overcome any natural fear and resistance to do important work?

What drives you?

- What will happen as a result of investing your time and energy in this project? Is it important to you? Is it important to your community? Is it important to the current state of the world?
- Why you? What unique perspective or experience do you bring to this work? If you don't have decades of experience or advanced degrees, do you care more than someone else? Will you work harder than someone else?
- Is it worth trying, even if it fails miserably?
- Why now? Will you regret not doing it in a year? Is there a reason why this is the perfect time? If

not now, when? Will next year be any different than this year?

- Are you pulling your hair out? Are you missing some answers? Do you need more information?

Have patience. It will serve you well on the rest of your journey.

CHAPTER 2

Define Your Roots

At the end of time I want my art to stand up and my
soul to bow down.
  —Rob Ryser, author of *Great Desires for Absent Things*

It was seven thirty on a cold Long Island winter night when
Amanda Wang arrived home from work.

She had been up since 4:30 A.M., practicing her training
routine for the Golden Gloves boxing competition, which was
two days away. She had run three miles first thing in the
morning and then she took the commuter train into Manhattan to train for three hours at the boxing gym before heading
to her job as a graphic designer. After working all day, she took
the commuter train back home and collapsed on her bed.

"As I lay there, motionless, feeling my head and muscles
throbbing, I began to cry; I still had to put in a three-mile run
in the dead of winter, all before dinner. I didn't want to move.

I thought if I pushed myself anymore, I'd make myself sick. I'd crack. I struggled to even put my running pants on. If I couldn't even put on my pants, how was I supposed to run three miles? I felt entitled to a little self-pity."

But she made herself put on her running pants and stepped outside, moving sluggishly at first, then slowly picking up speed and feeling her head clear.

As she tells it:

It was one of those winter nights where you can smell fireplaces through the cool and crisp air and see the moon peek through the clouds. I had my favorite music playing in the background, the one that centers me and makes me realize why running is good for my soul.

Then, in a quick moment, a memory came flooding back. It was the movie reel of my previous life— the one that culminated with a stint at the psychiatric hospital. There I was, rocking back and forth, all curled up in the bathroom of the psychiatric floor, wailing and crying for thirty minutes straight. I was in so much pain and confusion, so much fear and suffering that I constantly looked at the ceiling to see which beam could hold my weight.

I hadn't thought about that in some time, perhaps trying to block it out. It was the most painful, confusing, and lonely place I have ever been at, and I was both surprised and curious as to why the vivid memory had returned to me during my run. It seemed like such a long time ago. I can't even believe that was me, thinking where I am now. Back then I met eight of the nine criteria for borderline personality disorder; now I meet none.

But then I remembered that there were other people in that same moment (and some much worse) who felt as I had five years ago. People, like me, who don't know this diagnosis exists. People, like me, who don't know we could be taught a different way to live. People, like me, who don't know treatment could help put their lives back in order so that they could do the things they didn't even know they wanted to do in the first place.

Two miles into my run, I said to myself, "As bad as today was, as painful and exhausted as I felt today, it will never be as bad as that day in the bathroom five years ago. Look how far I've come that I can even do this—being able to transform my suffering into meaning." Pain cannot always be avoided. And in that moment, the physical pain lingered but the suffering went away.

In her recollection of this cold winter run, Amanda described the *root* of what motivates her to keep going: her mission as a mental health advocate for borderline personality disorder (BPD) patients, their families, and the physicians and therapists who serve them.

Amanda was diagnosed with BPD five years ago. Symptoms of BPD include self-doubt, self-injury, and frequent thoughts of suicide. Receiving appropriate treatment and medication has turned her life around. "My therapist told me that once you begin to get in recovery for BPD, you regain the will to live. But then you need to find a reason to keep living."

So she decided to train for the Golden Gloves and make a documentary film about the experience, called *The Fight Within Us*. The title signifies both the daily battle in her head between peaceful and disturbing thoughts, as well as the strength and courage within all of us to keep moving through adversity and get to a better place in our lives.

While many of Amanda's self-limiting beliefs come from her mental illness, everyone faces doubts and challenges while building a significant body of work.

Money, status, recognition, and fame are not enough.

We must tap into our deepest roots.

What are your roots?

Your roots are the purpose, beliefs, and convictions that provide the foundation for your body of work. They keep you strong and stable when you face challenges in your career and remind you why it is important to keep moving through adversity. They also provide depth and meaning to your creative process and remind you why it is important to chase the things you want to create.

Many people think their roots are in building a fortune. "I work for money. Money gives me the things that make me happy."

In my experience coaching all kinds of people over twenty years, I will tell you that money is not enough of a driver to make it through the truly challenging times. You will eventually face difficulties in every job or business that lead you to question if you have the strength to stick with your chosen career path.

When these moments appear, I like to ask the following questions:

- Why are you doing this (business) (parenting) (difficult project) (job)?
- What will happen if you succeed?
- Will it be worth it even if you fail?
- Why does it matter?
- What will you regret not doing?
- What will you rejoice leaving as a legacy at the end of your life?

No matter your current job or position, each person will have different answers to these questions depending on their specific roots: who they are, what they value, and what drives them.

Kelly Fiori makes a good living teaching martial arts to small children, teens, and adults. He is skilled at teaching kicks and punches and knows how to quiet a roomful of squealing kids in an instant. But if you ask him what is at the root of his work, his passion becomes visible on his face and resonates in his voice. "I don't want any child, anywhere, to suffer from bullying."

Erik Proulx is a filmmaker who is inspired by the city of Detroit. He made a documentary called *Lemonade: Detroit* about the rebirth of a city plagued by poverty. The city is a giant metaphor for the rebirth of anything we have written off, ignored, or feared. One of Erik's roots is that he understands the power of using creativity to comprehend and work through difficult, even impossible, situations.

Carlos Aceituno was a Guatemalan immigrant to San Francisco who loved Brazilian culture. He was a skilled music and martial arts teacher. He could really dance. But his root was using music to uplift, to heal, to strengthen, and to inspire communities. Kids who learned from him felt like family through the love that permeated his teaching, and adults felt their life force surge and spirits awaken by learning to play and dance Afro-Brazilian music. Carlos died unexpectedly at the age of forty-six, but the roots of his work continue to flourish in the community he taught and nourished.

To create a great body of work, you must first identify your roots. To make a strong and lasting impact, you must rely on them.

How do you identify your roots?

When you name your roots, just like Amanda did on that night when she felt like she could not muster the strength to put on her shoes, you remind yourself why your struggle is worth it in the long run if you want to create a significant body of work.

You discover your roots by reflecting on six primary questions:

1. What do you value?

Your values describe what is most important to you. They help guide you to make decisions and set boundaries around what you will accept in your life and career.

When you know your values, you can answer questions like:

- Should I take this job?
- Is this the right person to marry?

- Should I try this marketing approach in my business?
- Should I partner with this person?

When you make decisions in harmony with your values, you feel grounded and at ease.

When you make decisions in conflict with your values, you feel uneasy and ineffective.

Values can also be called character strengths.

> Example: You value critical thinking (thinking things through), honesty (authenticity, integrity), kindness (generosity, compassion), prudence (being careful about choices), and fairness (treating all people the same). You work for a financial institution that you know is engaged in unethical lending practices that prey on vulnerable communities. In this situation, no matter how much you try to make your job work, because the environment is in direct conflict with your values, you would be better served to look for an organization that is more aligned with your values.

2. What do you believe?

Your beliefs are unique to you and form the foundation for how you interpret and act in the world. They are shaped by your childhood, your life experiences, your education, advice you have received from teachers and mentors, and your philosophical or spiritual orientation. A simple way to understand what you believe is to answer the question "What do you know to be true?"

Example: One of your beliefs is that everyone, regardless of his or her background, has the capability to do great things.

3.   Why do you believe it?
Which experiences have shaped your values and your beliefs?

What has made you secure and certain in your values and beliefs?

Example: You believe that everyone, regardless of background, has the capability to do great things. You believe this because you watched your father, who came to this country as an immigrant in his early twenties, build a successful business with next to no money, even though he was not fluent in English.

4.   Whom do you care deeply about serving?
Of all the people who you could impact during your time on earth, whom do you want to work with? Which type of person "gets" you and really needs what you have to offer?

Example: You are a training and development manager with a humanities background, but you love to work with highly technical people. You appreciate their intelligence, curiosity, and critical perspective. You notice that when you teach them, you are pushed to deliver the highest quality, tested training classes. When you are able to earn their trust, you make a huge difference in their lives because they take what you teach and apply it methodically in their lives.

5.   Which problems do you want to solve?
Which challenges get you really fired up?

What impact do you want to have in the world?

What specific knowledge do you have that you think can make a difference in the world?

> Example: You are passionate about childhood nutrition. You notice that parents, especially moms, are so busy that they don't have time to plan and cook healthy meals. So you really want to help solve the childhood nutrition problem by discovering ways to support busy moms.

6. What drives you to act?

Most of us have long to-do lists. Very few of us can check off every item at the end of the day. What motivated you to accomplish great things in the past? What motivated you to finish? Pay special attention to thoughts, conditions, or techniques that cause you to take action.

> Example: You always wanted to run a marathon but constantly found excuses for not going through with it. Then your mother got breast cancer, and you suddenly felt inspired to run in a fund-raising marathon on her behalf. From this experience, you learn that you are inspired to take action when you see a direct benefit for someone you care about.

Don't sweat it if you can't answer all six of these questions yet. Simply plant the questions in your head and pay attention to the answers as they come to you.

As a career counselor, I have seen scores of people make themselves completely paralyzed looking for the "right answer" to their perfect vocation, or the meaning of their life. They believe that until they have the answer, they cannot move forward with anything else.

Viktor Frankl, in his stark and powerful book *Man's Search for Meaning*, provides the best antidote to this affliction:

> As each situation in life represents a challenge to man and presents a problem for him to solve, the question of the meaning of life may actually be reversed. Ultimately, man should not ask what the meaning of his life is, but rather he must recognize that it is *he* who is asked. In a word, each man is questioned by life; and he can only answer to life by *answering for* his own life; to life he can only respond by being responsible.

In April 2013, Amanda Wang showed her documentary about living with BPD, *The Fight Within Us*, at a mental health film festival in Washington, DC. "When people were watching my film, they were laughing, cheering, and screaming. It was a really wonderful experience to have them come up to me and say, 'Thank you for doing this because you've put a voice to what I've always experienced but never had the ability to share myself.' Hearing those words was very life affirming. They reminded me that what I'm doing on my mission is genuine and helpful to people."

Because Amanda defined her roots and remembered them at a point of great difficulty, she was able to create a deeply meaningful piece of her body of work and share it with those she cares about serving the most.

When I was in the middle of writing this book, I had a conversation with my kids, eight-year-old Josh and five-year-old Angela Rose (Rosie), on the way to school.

Josh: You should write your book at the office, Mom, not at home.

Me: I actually do write at the office too, but I also have to work with my clients to keep my business going. This will not last forever; I will be done with the writing in six weeks. Oh yeah, and then I will do two trips, to Portland and San Francisco.

Josh: Why do you have to go there?

Me: Because I need to spend time with my clients in person sometimes. Some moms choose to just spend their time with their kids, and that is their work. That is a great choice. Some moms, like me, want to spend time with their kids, *and* work outside the home. I want to leave something useful and important in the world with my work, which is why I am writing the book.

Rosie: I wish you were like the other kind of mom.

Me: I know that it really sucks sometimes. I know you have to sacrifice so much for this to happen. I hope that as you get older you might see things a little differently and think that it was worth it for me to spend time working.

Rosie: By the time you finish your book, we will be all grown up and we won't want to play with you anymore.

Me: I hope not!

As you can imagine, I felt like a deadbeat mom when I heard my kids say this. And at the same time, it was a chance to get very clear about my own roots.

What do I value?

I value love. And I value contribution, especially being able to be of assistance and counsel to others.

What do I believe?

I believe that it is vitally important to do things with my life that impact others in a positive way.

I believe that when people make great career choices that align their strengths and gifts with a deeper purpose, we all win. When we love what we do, we are more open and compassionate and better able to solve our biggest problems and challenges.

I believe that we are all equal, and each person on earth has something valuable to contribute, when given a good opportunity.

I believe that being a good parent is both spending time with my kids and perfecting my craft so that they see me engaged in work I love.

I believe that my kids are a huge priority in my life.

Why do I believe it?

I believe in making an impact on others because I have seen many of my clients' lives changed by the work we have done together. I have seen the joy on the face of a client who leaves a soul-sucking job and starts a successful business. I have beamed with pride, seeing clients grow their business or get great jobs or make inspiring films.

I believe people become more open and compassionate when they align their career goals with their strengths, because I have seen it happen hundreds of times. No longer gripped by negativity and creative angst, happily employed people become more interested in the world around them, are more willing to help others, and participate in activities that contribute to the greater good.

I believe that we are all equal and have something valuable to contribute, because I have worked with people from diverse economic, social, and ethnic backgrounds my entire life. I have learned valuable things from all of them.

I believe that being a good parent is both spending time with my kids and perfecting my craft, because I watched my dad be totally engaged and passionate about his work, and it had a massive influence on my own career choices.

I believe my kids are a huge priority in my life, because I watched my mom spend quality time and care shaping her children into responsible, kind, caring, and independent adults.

Whom do I care deeply about serving?

I care deeply about serving leaders in business who have huge potential and who may lack access to bigger stages and opportunities. I want to see them realize their potential and take their place in positions of leadership.

Why do I care about serving them?

I see the tremendous creativity and great results in work environments with diverse perspectives and experiences. I see the connection and joy that comes from watching people see leaders from all backgrounds.

What drives me to act?

I act when I see that I am at risk of not living according to my values. When my kids told me that they were tired of my spending all of my family time writing my book, I realized that I had better hurry up and finish.

Reflecting on my own roots reminds me that I must carefully choose the projects for my body of work that directly correlate to the problems I want to solve and affect those I want to help. I must constantly evaluate my priorities and choose only the projects that will have the biggest impact. If I don't, I am choosing to spend time away from my children for frivolous reasons.

Exercise: Identify Your Roots

Now it's your turn. Get to a place free of distraction. Take a deep breath, and answer these questions from the perspective of what you know to be true, not what you think you should say. There is no right answer, and your answers may change at different points in your career.

What do you value?

Brainstorm a list of values. Review the list, choose your top five values, and create a definition for each.

Value #1: _____

_____

Definition: _____

_____

Value #2: _____

_____

Definition: _____

_____

Value #3: _____

_____

Definition: _____

_____

Value #4: _____

_____

Definition: _____

_____

Value #5: _____

_____

Definition: _____

What do you believe?
List the top five things you know for sure about your life, yourself, your career, etc.

1. _____

_____

2. _____

_____

3. _____

_____

4. _____

_____

5. _____

_____

Why do you believe them?
Describe the key life experiences that have shaped your values and beliefs.

_____

_____

_____

_____

_____

Whom do you care deeply about serving?

Who are the people who you want to impact?

_____

_____

_____

_____

Why are they important to you?

_____

_____

_____

_____

_____

What will happen in their lives as a result of your support?

_____

_____

_____

_____

_____

Which problems do you want to solve?
What do you want to fix?

_____

_____

What could be made better in the world with your help?

_____

_____

What drives you to act?
Which thoughts, feelings, circumstances, or beliefs drive you to act?

_____

_____

_____

_____

When you get distracted, frustrated, stalled, or stuck while creating your body of work, revisit this section to remind yourself why it is important to keep going. Never forget your roots.

CHAPTER 3

Name Your Ingredients

> Everything you need to know you have learned through
> your journey.
>
> —Paulo Coelho, *The Alchemist*

For years, David Batstone and his wife dined regularly at an Indian restaurant near their home in the San Francisco Bay Area. A professor of Sustainable Business at the University of San Francisco and a longtime human rights advocate, David was shocked to learn that the owner of his favorite restaurant was a human trafficker.

"Unbeknownst to us, the staff at Pasand Madras Indian Cuisine who cooked our curries, delivered them to our table, and washed our dishes were slaves," he said.

As David recounted in his book *Not for Sale*, he learned the horrifying truth about the restaurant owner through a news story about two young women who were found unconscious in their apartment after they were poisoned by carbon monoxide leaking from a broken heating vent. After the police arrived on the scene, it was quickly revealed that the landlord, who was also the owner of the Indian restaurant, was a major human trafficker.

Overwhelmed with the horror in his own backyard, David was inspired to take off a year from his work as an investor and university professor to explore the issue of global human trafficking.

"I place a high value on curiosity," he said. "I thought, 'How can this happen, and how prolific is it in the world?' So I read everything I could get my hands on and spent a year visiting every continent to see human trafficking up close."

One stop on his global tour was northern Thailand, where he met a woman who had rescued twenty-seven children from the commercial sex trade. She was sheltering the kids in a hut built with palm leaves and a dirt floor. David said, "I was amazed by her courage and dedication. She had no plan, no support, and no infrastructure. And yet she had made a huge difference."

Moved to help, David took the most common first step of most humanitarian efforts. He founded a nonprofit called Not For Sale and raised funds to build a village to house the rescued children.

By the time he reached his fund-raising goal, the original twenty-seven kids had grown to one hundred and thirty.

The more he dug into the issue, the more David realized that new approaches were needed if human slavery was to be completely eradicated.

"Pulling drowning people out of a river is compassion. Justice is walking upstream to solve the reasons they are falling in," he said.

Drawing on his background in business and investing, the Not For Sale team began to work on social ventures to generate jobs and income in the communities most affected by human trafficking.

"For twenty-five years, I had a very bifurcated or tripolar existence. I had academic skills; I was an investor, working for a bank; I was a journalist; and I had human rights impulses to help the poor. My worlds were very separate. Until Not For Sale, I lived a siloed existence," he said. "When we have so many divergent interests, people often think we are unfocused, therefore ineffective. They buy into the 'specialty mode' ethos, where you are only valued if you have deep expertise in one area. I never saw my multiple interests as a problem. I saw the threads in my story. It was a natural, logical quilt. Not For Sale was the first time I could bring all of my worlds together— university professor, journalist, investor, and human rights activist."

While David's dedication to the cause of ending human slavery in this century is inspiring, it is his particular set of ingredients that make his work so effective.

What are ingredients?

We often describe ourselves primarily by the title of our profession or the name of our degree.

"This is Mike. He is an operations manager."

"This is Farah. She has a PhD from Harvard."

"This is Lee. She is a stay-at-home mom."

These descriptions communicate one aspect of our lives at

a particular point in time. But there are infinite other parts to each of us that add competence, distinction, emotional depth, strength, and meaning to the way we live each and every day.

I call these other parts our ingredients.

Our ingredients are the skills, strengths, experiences, identity, and knowledge that we have gained throughout the course of our lives.

They are what make us uniquely capable and interesting.

While Mike Bruny's business card might state that he is an operations manager for Intel, you may not know that he is also:

- A writer
- An encyclopedia of hip-hop lyrics
- Obsessed with bow ties
- A public speaker
- A brand ambassador
- Emotionally intelligent
- A student of lean startup principles
- African American
- A sports marketing expert
- A certified life coach
- The son of a mechanic and a housewife/babysitter/ seamstress

All of these ingredients make Mike a unique individual. (It may have been the combination of bow tie and emotional intelligence—plus his big smile—that made me spontaneously hug him the first time we met at the World Domination Summit in Portland, Oregon).

Mike uses his ingredients in many distinct ways to develop a rich and interesting body of work. He founded a bow-tie line. He teaches people the art of conference networking in online classes. He acts as a conference ambassador. He represents his company at events celebrating black men and women who work in the technology sector.

You must go beyond your job description

We highlight small elements of our skill set and experiences in order to fit in to a particular job description or business niche.

The reality is that in order to create your body of work you must rely on *all* of your ingredients, even those that you might not consider relevant to your professional career.

How do you determine your ingredients?

Your ingredients can be grouped into six main categories.

Roles

Which job roles have you fulfilled? (Examples: salesperson, parent, martial artist.)

Skills

Which measurable skills do you have? (Examples: Ruby on Rails programming, Spanish, customer service, accounting.) Where did you learn them?

Strengths

Which strengths come naturally to you? (Examples: writing, selling, baking.)

Experience

What kinds of work situations (academic, corporate, nonprofit, entrepreneurial) have you been in?

What kinds of life experiences have you had? (Examples: study abroad, travel, wealthy parents, abusive relationships, health challenges.)

Values

What do you believe in? (Examples: mastery, justice, Second Amendment rights.) Why?

Scars

Which life situations have brought you to your knees? What did you learn from those situations? (Examples: heartbreak, financial disasters, personal embarrassments, illness or injury.)

When I asked David Batstone to name his ingredients, he came up with the following list.

Roles

Journalist
Investor
Professor
Human rights activist
Father
Husband

Skills

Intuition
Pattern recognition

Vision of what could be rather than what is
Ability to empower others in times of fragmentation or crisis
Ability to identify talent
Storytelling
Personal discipline
Delayed gratification
Planning
Memory

Values
Social intelligence
Curiosity
Conviction around spiritual values

As we have seen in David's case, when you develop and integrate all of your available ingredients in your work, it becomes rich, deep, and very powerful.

In *Not for Sale*, David has created a strong antislavery movement by telling engaging stories, using his background in journalism. He has hired excellent staff, using his ability to identify talent. He has founded successful for-profit ventures (like REBBL tea) that benefit Not For Sale by using his investor and finance skills. He helps us diagnose and understand the incomprehensible horror of modern-day slavery, using his research in social enterprise. And he lives his conviction for spiritual values, a vision of what could be, and the discipline to get up every day and fight for justice for the most vulnerable people on earth.

Imagine what the world would be missing if David had followed the common belief that he should focus on only one small set of his ingredients in his work in order to succeed in his chosen field.

If your vision of your body of work involves a wide variety of jobs and passions, you will need to utilize your ingredients in many different ways and in different recipes.

How do you handle "unattractive" ingredients?

There are benefits to sprinkling ingredients like "Harvard graduate," "former editor at *Businessweek*," or "world-champion triathlete" onto your résumé or into your conversations. But what about the nonglamorous ingredients? Your losses, your failures, your past pain and suffering?

We've all been dealt some tough cards in our lives, some people far more than others.

No matter what the circumstances, your job is to create context and meaning around your ingredients so that you come at your body of work from a position of strength. We will talk a lot more about how to tell your story in chapter 9, so for now just focus on identifying and giving context to your complete list of ingredients.

There are three important parts to understanding your "unwanted" ingredients.

What lesson did I learn from this experience?

Some of my most powerful beliefs have come from negative experiences. My parents' divorce led me to develop inner strength, initiative, and independence. A horrible relationship in my twenties led me to set clear boundaries and to never let anyone speak to me in an abusive manner.

For each negative experience you have had in your life, ask

yourself, "What lesson did I learn from this experience?" These lessons become positive ingredients and sometimes your greatest strengths.

How does this lesson strengthen or reinforce my roots?

Challenging experiences are often the source of your roots.

Canadian entrepreneur Dan Martell became a millionaire in his midtwenties by selling his company, but he started his career with some tough circumstances.

"As a teenager, I grew up in a challenging environment. By the time I turned seventeen, I had been to jail twice for drug-related charges. At eighteen, I went to rehab and discovered computers. It saved my life. The reason Portage [rehab] worked for me was because all the staff were ex–drug addicts. They helped me climb out of a hole that they once found themselves in. That philosophy, that I learnt at an early age, is the reason why I spend so much time giving back. Getting support from those who've been through it before is why I've had success, in both business and in life."

This element of support from people who have been through it before is the core ingredient in Dan's latest venture, his website Clarity.fm, which connects entrepreneurs with questions to experts who have answers. Dan's vision is to reach a billion people in the next ten years with this "instant mentoring" startup.

After I glean the lesson and the root from this experience, how will I release the shame attached to it?

You may not find meaning or lessons in every unwanted ingredient. However, it is important to release any shame that comes from the experience, or it will hinder your ability to feel confident and powerful in your life.

Brené Brown is a shame and vulnerability researcher who wrote the bestselling book *Daring Greatly*. In the book, she describes a moment an audience member at her speaking engagement had a breakthrough about dealing with shame.

"I get it," he sighed.

"We all have shame. We all have good and bad, dark and light, inside of us. But if we don't come to terms with our shame, our struggles, we start believing that there's something wrong with us—that we're bad, flawed, not good enough—and even worse, we start acting on those beliefs. If we want to be fully engaged, to be connected, we have to be vulnerable. In order to be vulnerable, we need to develop resilience to shame."

Ingredients in a project-based world

In the new world of work, almost everything we do can be broken down into projects.

- The first ninety days of a new job is a project.
- The creation of a new product is a project.
- Producing an event is a project.

- Preparing for a promotion is a project.
- Conducting a fund-raising campaign for a non-profit is a project.
- Merging two companies is a project.

With each new project in your career, you have the opportunity to both leverage your diverse ingredients as well as develop new ones.

You don't have to use all your ingredients in every life situation. Each unique aspect of your life can be considered a recipe.

You can mix the skill of teaching, the experience of being a babysitter, and the values of love and stability in your recipe for being a good parent.

You can mix the skill of writing with the experience of being a marathon runner and the value of humor in your recipe for writing a book.

You can mix the skill of carpentry and your experience as a member of your church with your values of social justice in your recipe for volunteering with Habitat for Humanity.

HOW INGREDIENTS COME TOGETHER

Charlie Gilkey is a writer, business coach, former army logistics officer in the Iraq War, and PhD candidate in philosophy. He writes at productiveflourishing.com. He wrote this essay to describe how his ingredients of "entrepreneur," "warrior," and "philosopher" fit together.

. . . . . .

One of the questions that has come from a lot of my interviews lately is about how my background of philosophy, military service, and entrepreneurship converges. I've always been intrigued by that question, largely because of how many preconceptions people have about each of the three.

Specifically, though, people have found the most tension between my military and philosopher identities. It normally goes like this: "How does a *philosopher* end up in the *army*?" Deconstruction: How does a cerebral, abstract thinker end up in the dirty, practical profession of military leadership?

I'm sure it won't be the last time I'll say it, but here goes: My mission is really to advance human "flourishing." The way that I understand philosophy is that it's the search for understanding how to thrive in the world, at both the personal and societal level. It's not just what it means for *me* to flourish and how to do it but what it means for *us* to flourish and how we might go about that. Last, it's been my experience, observation, and reflection that *most* of what really matters isn't a matter of knowing, but, rather, taking meaningful action on the stuff that matters.

If you're really out to advance human flourishing, there's an unfortunate fact of the world that you must come to grips with: it so turns out that, *in this world*, there's a lot of human suffering. To countervail those forces, you need a wide mixture of responses—social, political, religious, economic, *and* military.

At the same time, different conditions require different responses.

I understand that there are considerable differences of thought on this issue and I've spent nigh two decades preparing for it, living it, or reflecting about it—but being a warrior and being a philosopher aren't as incompatible as many make it seem. Just as there are many ways to be a doctor or a teacher, there are many ways to be a warrior and a philosopher. The simplified stereotypes we receive or perpetuate rob of us of the richness of understanding we may get to upon further reflection.

My time in the military has passed—I've long since "laid down that shield"—yet the warrior in me is still alive and thriving. The more I'm removed from my prior service, the prouder, honored, and appreciative I become of it. I understand how critical every bit of it has led me to where I am.

> If philosophy addresses the *why* of what I do, my
> military service and my current profession addresses
> *how* I go about doing that. My field of action is now
> more directly social and economic since I see that it's
> the best fit for my talents and mission. There's a high
> degree of transference of skills and perspectives from
> what I've done before to what I'm doing now.

Exercise: Determine Your Ingredients

Step 1: Assess your ingredients.
Brainstorm answers in each of the six categories of ingredients:

Roles
Which job roles have you fulfilled?

Skills
Which measurable skills do you have? Where did you learn them?

Strengths
Which strengths come naturally to you?

Experience
What kinds of work situations have you been in?

What kinds of life experiences have you had?

Values

What do you believe in? Why?

Scars

Which life situations have brought you to your knees?

What did you learn from those situations?

Step 2: Build context around your ingredients.

Review your list and highlight:

Which ingredients are you most excited by and proud of?

Which ingredients do you want to use in your next project?

Which ingredients do you feel embarrassment or shame about?

Answer these three questions about those ingredients that cause you to feel shame:

1. What lesson did I learn from this experience?

2. How does this lesson strengthen or reinforce my roots?

3. After I glean the lesson and the root from this experience, how will I release the shame attached to it?

Step 3: Determine the ingredients you are excited to learn next.

Which skills do you want to learn?

What experience do you want to gain?

Which new project could you create that would allow you to develop specific ingredients?

Your ingredients are going to play a critical role in the remaining parts of this book as you begin to build your body of work by choosing a work mode, creating and innovating, surfing your fear, collaborating, establishing your definition of success, and selling your story. Hold tight to your ingredients and be proud of what makes you unique.

To see examples of people's ingredient lists, including creative ways to describe and display them, go to pamelaslim .com/bodyofwork and click on the "Ingredients" chapter.

CHAPTER 4

Choose Your Work Mode

But I say to you that when you work you fulfill a part of earth's furthest dream, assigned to you when that dream was born,

And in keeping yourself with labor you are in truth loving life,

And to love life through labor is to be intimate with life's inmost secret.

—Khalil Gibran, *The Prophet*

I was standing in a dusty courtyard in an improvised city on the outskirts of Bogotá, Colombia, spinning a four-year-old child upside down. He was giggling, which made the other eighty kids in line giggle too. After three spins, I put him down, he ran to the back of the line, and the next kid stepped up and jumped into my arms.

At that moment, as much as I loved swinging eighty cute

Colombian kids in circles every morning, I wondered if my true career path was as an expatriate aid worker.

It was my senior year in college, and I was completing my bachelor's degree in international service and development, with a focus in nonformal adult education. I had always had a passion for grassroots development and social change. I loved the people and culture of Latin America, so I planned on having a career living abroad.

But the more I studied the field and got direct experience with it by interning in development projects, the more I felt that my role was not as an expatriate aid worker (which is better served by host nationals) but rather should be in my own country, supporting change from within.

Starting at age twenty, I became obsessed with the Afro-Brazilian martial art form of capoeira. After training hard for a year, I took over as volunteer executive director of Omulu Capoeira Group in the Bay Area, and for the next ten years I ran the organization, including its marketing, grant writing, fund-raising, program development, and public relations. We started a youth program, Community Action Project, with one student, Jimmy Jarquin, and over the next number of years, partnering with more than twenty youth service organizations in the area, grew it to two hundred kids. I co-taught a class at San Francisco State University in the Dance Ethnology department with my teacher, Mestre Preguiça. We took groups of students on study tours to Brazil, where we visited capoeira schools all over the country.

Upon graduation from college, I took a job as a program assistant for the Marin Community Foundation, a large foundation endowed with millions of dollars. In that role, I got to see how many different organizations were structured and funded, and learned about philanthropy.

Wanting to get my feet wet in direct service, my next job was at the Exploratorium, a San Francisco art and science museum that I had loved since I was a child. I worked in the teacher-training program and got to see the design and delivery of a program up close.

My next leap was into software training and development, in an "only in San Francisco" firm that was owned by a commune and operated out of Victorian homes in the Haight-Ashbury district. It was there that I was exposed to corporate software training and had my first peek into the field of training and development. I opened the South of Market training facility, then ran the backend of the training business.

When the company began to falter, I moved to Wells Fargo Nikko Investment Advisors, which after a merger became Barclays Global Investors. It was my first experience in a purely corporate environment, and I loved it. I gazed out at the San Francisco skyline from the twenty-ninth floor and treasured my fresh pencils and endless supply of Post-it Notes. I worked in training and development, and I loved learning new things every day from the financial traders, analysts, and administrative staff. I built management and technical training programs to keep pace with explosive staffing growth and took advantage of learning all about corporate training and development from my bosses and exceptionally gifted mentors.

But, quite suddenly, when I turned thirty and got pneumonia (perhaps from ten years of working ninety-plus-hour weeks), I decided to quit my job cold turkey. August 15, 1996, was the last time I collected a paycheck as a corporate employee.

For the next nine years, I worked as a management consultant in some of the most well-known organizations in the world. I worked in every kind of workplace situation you can imagine, from helping organizations grow (during boom cycles) to helping them shrink (during downturns). I worked with senior executives, frontline managers, salespeople, engineers, and designers. I would joke with my clients that there was an endless need for my services, since as soon as you put more than one person together in a company you had a dysfunctional organization.

After so many invigorating years as a consultant in larger organizations and seeing how many corporate employees were dying to quit their jobs to start a business, I was ready to work with individual clients. I trained as a coach with Martha Beck and began to think about making the transition from consultant to coach.

When I met my husband and moved to Arizona, we knew we wanted to have kids, so I didn't want to be on the road all the time as a consultant. After my son was born, I took a class on online marketing with Suzanne Falter, and built my online platform, which became the Escape from Cubicle Nation blog, book, and coaching business. Over eight years, I coached people all over the world in their transition from employee to entrepreneur. I began to speak at conferences, write books, and work with corporate partners to develop content for the small-business market.

In retrospect, and truly without a plan, I realized that I had covered just about every work mode: nonprofit volunteer, nonprofit employee, small-business employee, corporate employee, stay-at-home mom, freelancer, consultant, small-business owner, and independent producer.

Since I have gotten tremendous growth and satisfaction from each of these work modes, I believe very strongly that there is no one right way to work; there is only the path that brings you great satisfaction and allows you to build a body of work that you are proud to share with the world.

Learning about different work modes will give you more stability and a wider variety of options in an increasingly uncertain global economy.

Work modes in the new world of work

The last twenty years have brought massive revolution to the way we work. Where telecommuting was a novelty a decade ago, now entire industries have sprung up around Internet business models that have customers, suppliers, and producers distributed all over the world.

In a study conducted by software company Intuit in 2010 and cited by NextSpace CEO Jeremy Neuner, it is predicted that by 2020, more than 40 percent of the U.S. workforce will be so-called contingent workers. That is more than 60 million people.

In a twenty-first-century economy, people move between many organizations, jobs, and business environments. Change, flux, and continual upheaval are the new normal.

But most people are not aware of the many ways they can apply their various talents to different work modes in order to earn a living while creating a meaningful body of work.

A laid-off corporate employee may have highly valuable skills that he can use to work on freelance projects while he looks for a new full-time position. A worn-out small-business owner may not realize that her skills could be extremely valuable within a larger organization, where she could put them to use without continually hustling for new customers, and feel the relief of a regular paycheck.

This list of work modes will continue to grow and evolve with innovations and changes in the economy:

Employee
> You work for someone else for a wage and benefits.

Contractor
> You work for yourself, or for an agency, often for a primary employer or project.

Freelancer
> You work for yourself, doing a variety of projects for a variety of clients.

Small-Business Owner
> You own a specific online or brick-and-mortar business, where you develop and sell products and services to a specific market.

Startup Founder with Funding
> You develop a specific product with great market potential and go after angel or venture-capital funding.

Social Entrepreneur
> You own a business that has an explicit social agenda, often using the profits, or a portion of profits, generated by the enterprise to fund projects that support social good.

Independent Producer

You are an artist (including fine arts, photography, music, writing, and more), and you raise funds through a combined source of crowd-sourcing (like Kickstarter or Indiegogo), or by selling your wares on sites like Bēhance or Etsy. You may also be lucky enough to have a patron, or a corporate sponsor.

Nonprofit Professional

You are a freelancer or an employee of a non-profit organization.

Unofficial Confederation Member

In the new world of work, many independent professionals, such as coaches, Web developers, programmers, writers, and graphic designers, gather together to work on projects, in addition to work they do independently. Often there is no official business or organization structure, just deep trust and confidence in each other's abilities, and sales capability within the confederation to pitch big projects.

Internet Personality

The rise of advertising on YouTube has opened the door for individuals with compelling (depending on who you ask) personalities. The *New York Times* estimates that Jenna Marbles, who they called "The Woman With 1

Billion Clicks," could have earned as much as $346,827.12 in 2012.

Multipotentialites

As a coach for many hundreds of clients, I noticed that there was a certain kind of person who not only had a huge amount of unique "ingredients" but who also felt extremely boxed in whenever we would talk about choosing a particular kind of career or business or work mode.

Thanks to Emilie Wapnick, I now know that these folks are called multipotentialites.

Emilie coined the term to refer to a person who has many interests and talents and often works in a mixture of the work modes previously described.

As she describes it on her website, putty like.com:

You've spent your whole life flitting from interest to interest, maybe pursuing a handful of projects at any one time. You've owned a catering business, worked at a medical clinic, trained dogs, taught yoga, played cello in a chamber group. . . .

All of this jumping around has felt amazing. But if you stop to ponder your path for too long, it starts to worry you. . . .

And then you discover that you are a multipotentialite.

Suddenly it all makes sense. You realize that you are not broken or noncommittal or afraid of your own success. The reason you can't find your One True Calling is because you don't have a singular calling, you have many. The zigzagging, the sporadic obsessions, the weird interdisciplinary projects, they all now fit now. They make sense.

If you fit in this category (which makes me chuckle, since I know that many multipotentialites do not like to be put in one category), know that you will most likely be experimenting with many different work modes.

Your body of work may be a bit more eclectic and diverse than those with a more singular craft or career focus.

Knowing when to switch work modes: the loathing scale

In my work with corporate clients who want to leave their job to start a business, I often make reference to a *loathing scale.*

This is a quick indicator of how critical it is to make short-term plans to leave a job, versus staying on a more long-term path.

Remember that your journey doesn't have to end with your starting your own business. The loathing scale can also be used to determine when you need to change positions, companies, or industries.

Imagine a ruler from one to ten. One is the low end, and ten is the high end.

The chill range: one to four

In the chill range, you may not be in the best possible job for your skills, but there are a lot of things you like about it. You can comfortably see staying in your job for one to two years as you slowly work on your side business.

The danger of the chill range is that you may be lulled into staying somewhere comfortable for many years if you aren't given enough incentive to change your situation.

The angst range: five to eight

There are a lot of things that bother you in the angst range. You may not like your job. Or the company culture. Perhaps you have a really bad boss. Or you are killing yourself working extra hours and it is eating into family or social time.

Physically, you notice your energy goes up and down. You have some high-energy good days when you get stuff done, but overall you feel from slightly annoyed to highly stressed when you head to the office.

In this range, you want to take your side business plans seriously, since small changes in your job can push you from the angst to the run-screaming stage.

The run-screaming range: nine to ten

People in the run-screaming range feel physically sick walking into their office building. Symptoms include low energy, depression, high blood pressure, frequent respiratory illnesses, or other stress-related symptoms.

It is very difficult to work on a side business in this range, since you are either so exhausted or so angry that your best creative work doesn't flow.

Obviously, this is not a scientific test, so you will need to do a lot of reflection to see which range feels the most accurate for your situation.

But if you find yourself on the high end of the loathing scale, chances are you will either shut down physically (by getting really sick), throw red staplers in a rage while screaming obscenities in the middle of a company meeting (otherwise known as losing your mind), or get yourself fired (the essential self is very effective at inciting poor performance if it feels under attack or threatened).

Even if you are planning on starting a business in the long run, you may want to take an interim step by changing jobs or companies if you are not in a financial place where you are able to earn your full income yet in your new business.

Hating your job intensely is not a business plan or a life plan.

The body doesn't lie. Pay attention to the loathing scale.

Expand your comfort zone

Isn't it wonderful to get to a place in your business or career where you don't have to struggle so much every day to make a happy, healthy living?

Jim Collins calls it the "sweet spot," and Martha Beck calls it the "Promised Land" in her four-square model of change.

I call it dangerous.

If you don't pay attention, one of two things will happen:

- Without challenge, the competence you have worked so hard to develop will soon become boring and stale, leading to dissatisfaction.

- Without notice, you will get laid off or the market will fall, and because you have gotten too comfortable, you won't have an adequate backup plan.

I don't mean to sound like an alarmist, but before you start to creep up on the loathing scale, you need to start to expand your comfort zone.

My friend Michele Woodward has a definition of growth that I like better than "get outside of your comfort zone." She calls it "expanding your comfort zone."

If you are a small-business owner, are you ready to stretch yourself and grow your market base or business model? If you are an employee, are you ready for a new challenge?

How do you know when you are ready?

• You look at the content you have created and realize that many more people could use it than the market you are currently serving.

• You are a bit fatigued at putting all your energy into the "build it and they will come" model of content marketing and are ready for some bigger moves.

• You have built significant visibility and trust in your market or workplace.

• You have your basic business operations and systems in place, and have a clean and efficient way of serving your current customers.

Questions to ask yourself to help find new markets (assuming they are aligned with your roots and that you can really put your ingredients to work)

• Is there a **larger company** that serves my market and has something that would truly help my customers grow and develop?

• Is there something **I have to offer a larger company** that serves their market and could offer a significant value to their customers?

• Are there opportunities in **government contracts** that I could take advantage of because of interest, affiliation, or business designation? (For example, woman-, veteran-, or minority-owned, et cetera—you can find detailed information here: http://www.sba.gov/category/navigation-structure/contracting /contracting-opportunities.)

• Is there a **nonprofit organization or cause** that is aligned with my core business that I could serve with my skills or contacts, and that could expose me to new peers or partners?

• If I work primarily in online business, are their **local businesses or organizations** that could use my expertise or services, perhaps in a live configuration instead of an online one?

• Would I consider **selling my business**? If so, what should I begin to prepare?

What to expect people will ask for when you start to grow markets

When you start to reach out into new markets, particularly with larger partners, you need to frame the story of your business in a new way. You need to prepare:

• **Statistics** that demonstrate your market reach (Twitter followers, blog readers, newsletter subscribers, Facebook fans, total number of customers served, annual sales, et cetera).

• **A succinct vision** of your business that describes what you are about and what makes you unique, how you have grown your business to this stage, where you plan to go in the next twelve to twenty-four months, whom you want to partner with and why.

• **A powerful story** that gets partners excited about the business vision. Why are you excited about growing your business (beyond making money)? Lauryn Ballesteros, who has worked to secure large partnerships for Seth Godin's Domino Project and Squidoo, told me that a passionate, compelling story is a huge part of successful sponsor sales.

• **A path of trust and credibility.** Who can vouch for you? What do your customers say about you? What do peers and mentors think about your work? What does Google pull up with your name in the search box? Now is a great time to galvanize your community behind you so that your growth benefits everyone in your ecosystem, not just your own business.

Moving from one work mode to the next

In the old world of work, we described specific career paths, such as doctor, lawyer, entrepreneur, or writer.

In today's world of work, due to either personal choice or circumstances outside of your control, there is a great chance that you will change your work mode at least once in your career. More likely multiple times.

The era of the side hustle

A few years ago, my friend's teenage daughter informed her that she was enrolling in a nail-technician class at high school.

The friend, who has been prepping her daughter for a good college education since she was a toddler, was less than thrilled.

"Why are you taking a beauty-school class instead of an advanced-placement academic class? Wouldn't that be better for college?"

"*Mom*," she said in an exasperated tone that only teenagers do perfectly, "doing nails is my **side hustle** to help pay for college. I can do it anytime, in the dorms, and there is a ready market if I need some extra cash."

My friend went from worry to admiration for the enterprising spirit of her daughter.

We all need a side hustle.

If you are still working in a corporate job, a side hustle is a great way to test and try new business ideas. It can also be part of your backup plan in case you lose your job. Examples of side hustles I have seen from corporate employee clients and friends over the years:

- Web design
- Home organizing
- Writing and editing
- Computer maintenance
- Massage
- Tax preparation
- Yoga
- Catering
- Photography

A good side hustle will have the following characteristics:

- You enjoy doing it.
- You are good at it.
- You are very clear about who your market is (for example, if you are good with computers, you could offer your services to other homeowners in your neighborhood on your community bulletin board or in a newsletter).
- You can generate a decent amount of quick cash in a short period of time.
- It does not require an extensive website or ongoing brand-building efforts like a more substantial small business. But more substantial businesses can and do emerge from side hustles.
- It will not get you thrown in jail (dealing crack,

while profitable and possible from your home, is
not recommended).

The side hustle does not only apply to corporate employees;
it can also be a great backup for small-business owners affected
by shifting markets or slow sales.

During the decade I spent as a consultant developing and
delivering programs and management training for corporations, I met many hardworking employees with no contingency
plan in the off chance they were laid off one day.

I always encouraged them to change their mind-set and
adopt my mantra: "We are all self-employed." Even if they intended to stay in the corporate world, I explained, they'd be
safer if they viewed their employer as a client.

A side hustle is a form of career insurance.

Even if you're happy in your career, you want to have a
backup plan in case you hit a bumpy stretch of road. It's also a
way to experiment with new ideas and fields, keeping your
brain fresh and active, and it can provide a financial cushion,
bringing in extra revenue for whatever goal you deem important, from paying down debt to saving for a vacation or bolster-
ing your retirement account.

In today's work world, you never know when your job may
change dramatically or completely vanish. In order to prepare
for the unexpected and continue to develop your interests and
skills, always have at least one side hustle. Not only will it help
pad your bank account, but you will be able to strengthen your
all-important list of ingredients and broaden your body of
work.

How to prepare for a side hustle

From a sales perspective, all you need to kick-start your side hustle is a clear description of your product or service, a place where people can buy what you're selling (like a website), and a way to get paid (like PayPal or Square).

You'll want to be sure not to run afoul of state and local laws for small businesses where you live. Most local government small-business associations can help you avoid such problems.

The free nonprofit resource SCORE will also assist you. Check out score.org to find a mentor.

Steps to launch a side hustle

These are the key steps you'll need to take to set up a side hustle.

• Choose a legal structure for your business. In the United States, most people with side hustles operate them as sole proprietors or limited liability corporations (LLCs), but there may be a reason to choose a different structure, such as an S or C corporation. A SCORE mentor can help you figure out which legal structure is best for you and explain how to create it.

• Get any necessary business licenses and permits. The U.S. Small Business Administration's website (sba.gov) can walk you through the process.

• Set up a business bank account. Even if you have a tiny side business, it is best to keep that money separate from your personal bank account.

• Check to see if you need business insurance. Some professions require liability insurance. If you need coverage, you can probably get it for a reasonable monthly fee. Read the U.S. Small Business Administration website's primer on business insurance for details (http://www.sba.gov/content/business-insurance).

• Check with a CPA to learn the tax requirements. You'll want to know which expenses are deductible as well as when and how to file your business taxes.

Three potential side hustle dangers
Although I'm a huge proponent of side hustles, you need to watch out for these potential problems.

1. Violation of employment policies. If you're a full-time employee, check with your employer before starting a side hustle to be sure you're not prohibited from outside work. You don't want to do anything that could jeopardize your job.

2. Overcommitment. Be careful not to take on so much side work that you become stressed and overwhelmed.

3. Planning too much, doing too little. A side hustle is a way to have fun trying something new. If you find yourself creating a thirty-page business plan, you're missing the point.

Start small. Then, once you see real promise developing, you can invest more effort planning and expanding.

Wading into entrepreneurial waters with a side hustle can be exciting, invigorating, and lucrative. Better still: if you wind up with the misfortune of being handed a cardboard box and twenty minutes to pack, you'll breathe easier knowing that you have a backup plan ready to go.

FREELANCE AND VIRTUAL ASSISTANT SITES

More and more sites are popping up to offer side-hustle employment opportunities to freelancers and to provide talent to global organizations of all sizes.

Freelance Sites
Craigslist—craigslist.org

Freelancer—www.freelancer.com

FreelanceSwitch—http://freelanceswitch.com

Gorkana Jobs alerts: www.gorkanajobs.com/alerts

Guru—www.guru.com

oDesk—www.odesk.com

Thumbtack—www.thumbtack.com

Virtual Assistant Sites
eaHELP—www.eahelp.com

Get Friday—www.getfriday.com

Hire My Mom—http://hiremymom.com

International Virtual Assistants Organization—www.ivaa.org

Online Business Manager—http://online businessmanager.com

VAnetworking—www.vanetworking.com

Virtual Assistants—http://virtualassistants
.com

Designer and Developer Sites
Smashing Jobs (via *Smashing Magazine*)—http://
jobs.smashingmagazine.com

37signals—http://jobs.37signals.com

Artist Sites
Bēhance—www.behance.net

Etsy—www.etsy.com

Writing Sites
Morning Coffee—www.freelancewriting
.com/newsletters/morning-coffee-freelance
-writing-jobs.php

Problogger—http://jobs.problogger.net

Because the Web continually changes and
grows, this is a partial list. For an updated
list, and to suggest sites I have missed, visit
pamelaslim.com/bodyofwork.

The more time goes on, the more diversity we will see in
work modes, work flexibility, and multiple-pronged career paths.

I want to stress two very important points, as you think about your body of work:

1. The world of work is not stable. You cannot count on any one work mode to deliver ongoing creative and financial stability.

2. Even if you *choose* to stay in one field, or with one company, be prepared to have a backup plan. Start a side hustle. Investigate freelance options. Share your body of work with a much bigger audience through a website or blog. And make sure that you have a cross-pollinated network so if you need to make a leap, you will have a net of people to catch you.

Exercise: How to Explore and Switch Work Modes

In my work with *Escape from Cubicle Nation*, I have seen people make dramatic shifts in their careers. Kelly Newsome went from lawyer to yoga teacher and women's wellness expert, and Ivan Martinez went from sales and marketing manager to professional photographer.

If you want to try a new work mode in order to build your body of work, answer these questions.

What are the rules of the game?

Which skills, ingredients, experience, certifications, or education are required to be successful in this work mode?

How do people get hired? Is there a clear, objective hiring process, or do you have to have the right connections?

Are there any deal killers, like age limits or physical restrictions? (No matter how much you want it, you may not be able to switch work modes from fifty-five-year-old computer pro-grammer to NBA draftee. Then again, I would love to be proven wrong.)

How do I need to tell my story to get hired?

In a traditional job, you may need to have a strong résumé and cover letter, with a LinkedIn profile.

In a freelance job, you may need to have a place to house your portfolio, as well as testimonials or ratings from satisfied past clients.

What story will resonate most with the new market? (We'll discuss this more in chapter 9.)

Who can I talk to who has been successful in this work mode?

The best way to learn the true ins and outs of a work mode is to talk to a handful of people who are currently doing it exceptionally well. It is very important to get up-to-date information, since someone's experience as a freelancer, or Internet personality, or employee five years ago may be very different from the reality of today's market.

CHAPTER 5

∽

Create and Innovate

But unless we are creators we are not fully alive.

What do I mean by creators? Not only artists, whose acts of creation are the obvious ones of working with paint or clay or words. Creativity is a way of living life, no matter our vocation or how we earn our living.

—Madeleine L'Engle, *Walking on Water*

When Mike Carson was nine years old, he begged his parents to buy him a digital video camera that could add special effects like explosions and flying helicopters. He was obsessed with film and proudly produced his first video, starring his little brother, within a week of getting the camera.

Through the rest of grammar school and junior high, Mike learned everything he could about filming, special effects, and editing by watching YouTube tutorials. He even found a way to use his video skills for most of his school projects. By his early teens, he was making videos for his dad's nonprofit organization.

In high school, he developed an affinity for music and loved discovering new artists. "I grew up listening to music in church and my parent's music in the house. But it was fun to find my own taste." He became a big Kanye West fan in 2004 after hearing his first album, *The College Dropout*. In 2008, when Mike was sixteen, he went to see Kanye live in concert and was blown away by his production and creativity.

Turning to his friend at the concert, he said, "We have to work with this guy sometime!"

Two years later, he was sitting in a studio in Australia, filming Kanye West and Jay Z during the making of their platinum album, *Watch the Throne*.

"To this day, that is the craziest moment I have ever had in my life," Mike said. "I'm eighteen years old, holding a camera, watching my favorite two artists in the world make an album in front of me."

How did he get there?

After high school, Mike enrolled in Columbia College with a major in television editing. He assumed he would follow a traditional path and get his college degree before finding a job in television.

During his freshman year he met Mike Bowen (Mike B.), a fellow Columbia College student who was working at RSVP Gallery, a local store in Chicago. The store's owner was also Kanye West's manager and creative director, and after learning about Mike C.'s video skills, he gave him some small creative projects to do for the store.

The Mikes, as they came to be known, started to work on the side on freelance video projects for emerging artists. One such client was Big Sean, a relatively unknown rapper at the time, signed to Kanye West's GOOD Music label. They made a music video for him and it caught the attention of Kanye's team.

"We were in the right place at the right time," said Mike C.

Since Mike C. was still in college, his parents, while excited for him, didn't want him to make the decision to leave school without some serious thought. He finally decided that he could not pass up the opportunity, and quit school.

Over the next two years, the Mikes would work on a variety of projects, including the Kanye and Jay Z collaboration in Australia.

"We took it all in," said Mike C. "We watched every aspect of how Kanye ran his business. I learned about music, editing, fashion, stage production, and promotion."

In addition to his other clients, Mike C. became the creative director for Big Sean. He handled tours, album packaging, and merchandising. He produced a show in Detroit in a stadium for thirteen thousand people. He handled every part of the production: set design, video, staging, and promotion. The show was a big success.

Not yet twenty years old, the Mikes moved to Los Angeles and expanded their creative empire.

Now their hip-hop blog, *Illroots*, gets more than a million hits a month. In their creative business, they work with advertisers and artists to create videos and produce live events.

"I am so excited by the possibility of producing tours," said Mike C. "I saw how Kanye treated his shows like Broadway productions. Right now, I wake up every day and learn something new. I read, watch videos, study people, experiment with different mediums, and try to be a better person every day. As much as you might think that the lifestyle of the people I have worked with is crazy, it is really not. They are focused on always growing, always moving, always pushing the edge. I want to be surrounded by people like that. I do eventually want to go back to school and complete my degree. But it won't be in film or video, because I am learning all of that now. I want to keep living, keep creating, and keep progressing in my skills every day. Most importantly, I want to make my parents proud."

You may think that Mike's story is about a one-in-a-million chance of getting a big break by being discovered by someone famous.

It is not.

Mike's story is about an eighteen-year old kid who mastered the most important skill of his era: creating innovative work that opens the door to opportunity.

The skill of creating

In the new world of work, our ability to create a powerful body of work is what will determine our ongoing employability. In order to create, you have to quickly scope, design, and ship a series of creative projects that come in many forms.

• If you step into a new job, you have a short time to make a mark and prove to your employer that he or she made a great choice hiring you.

• If you start a business, you have a limited amount of time to get a product to market and attract your first customers.

• If you run a nonprofit, you need to organize a program or a project to serve your community and galvanize funding.

• If you merge two companies, you have to evaluate staffing, manage customers, work on branding, integrate the cultures, and create a unified business plan.

Your creative work will tell your story. And in order to tell a story, you have to get it out of your head and into the world.

As Scott Belsky, the author of *Making Ideas Happen* and founder of Bēhance and 99U, says about the future of work:

"We will ultimately live in a perpetual data-driven talent edition. Everything you create will be measured and tracked by others through comments, shares, and likes. Your work will come up on the radar of potential employers and clients, and the data will tell them if you are worth talking to or hiring."

Every creative project must answer the following questions:

What do you want to create?
Name it. Describe it.

(A book, a job, a video, an app)

Who is it for?
Describe your audience.

(Include specific details about who you are targeting.)

Why does it need to be accomplished?
Describe the roots of the project.

(How does this fit into your body of work? Who will be affected by it? What positive outcomes will occur as the result of you completing it?)

How are you going to structure the project?

Define a model.

(Who has done something similar in the past? How was it structured? How can you customize this model and make it your own?)

When does it need to be finished?

Make a timeline. Set a deadline.

(Nothing happens without a deadline. Set a date and work backward.)

Soon enough, asking these questions will become second nature. You will think about each one for each new piece of your body of work. Creating rapidly will quickly become an unconscious skill.

Your creative process

Everyone has an opinion about the best way to accomplish creative work.

Some advocate a daily writing practice, starting first thing in the morning.

Others think you should work from 9:00 P.M. to 2:00 A.M. on your creative projects if you really want to "crush it."

I can't think without a clean desk.

If you need to stuff your face with Nutella while you edit videos, or like to have paper stacked twenty inches high around your computer while you code, or want to mess around on Facebook while you write, go ahead and do it.

Whatever you prefer, you must make sure your setting allows you to create consistently on a sustainable basis.

Your creative process is your own, and no one is allowed to touch it, but make sure that you know yourself and how you can best fashion an environment that supports your work.

Research the best methods and choose one that works for you. If you want to get work done, you must claim your creative process.

Scott Belsky says that in all the years he has been writing and speaking about taking action and managing a creative business, the one piece of advice that helps the most people is to "tell people about what you are working on, especially when it feels immature or you worry about someone stealing it. You get priceless feedback. If it is a bad idea, you get an amount of accountability. Tell people, 'Here is what I am working on. It is launching in three months.' Then you will have to sweat it out to launch in three months."

There Are Four Parts to Your Creative Process

Part one: Enjoy the adventure of your craft
Part two: Develop a mastery mind-set
Part three: Scope, test, scope, test
Part four: Flex your creative muscles

Let's explore each one in some depth.

Part one: Enjoy the adventure of your craft
I was pretty fearless in my teens and twenties.

I figured out how to get myself to Switzerland as an exchange student at sixteen, with little money and no contacts.

I had many adventures in college in Mexico and Colombia, often traveling alone and having some dangerous experiences, like being held up at knife point and walking home alone after a late night of salsa dancing (sorry, Mom).

I lived in Rio de Janeiro for six months by myself while I trained in the Afro-Brazilian martial art of capoeira.

And much earlier in my life, as soon as I really got the hang of books, I loved to read stories of myths and adventures from all over the world.

I think intense devotion to your craft is a commitment to going on a hair-raising adventure.

Unfortunately, we often focus too much on the outcome of our creative projects instead of the fun, and often painful, process of bringing them to life.

As a wide-eyed first-time author who was struggling to put pen to paper, I got some great advice from the publisher of my first book:

"Write the damned book," he said.

And now having *written* the damned book (two, actually), I will tell you that it was an adventure to the grandest scale of my childhood dreams. I fought demons. I interviewed kings and queens. I scaled the highest mountains of impossibility, gave up, died, and somehow came back to life in time to finish the last chapter. All while changing tiny baby diapers, managing play dates, serving clients, and dealing with economic warfare all around me.

I think craft has spirit.

In individual sessions with clients, writing on my own, or in a large room teaching a group of people, there are moments of intense and utter grace.

They come when you immerse yourself in your work and feel like you have to know how to do it better or else you will lose your quest and the king will behead you in the public square.

They come when you feel ideas rising up in your chest and you know, for certain, that they are turning into something big and powerful, as if conjured by a magic spell.

Craft is not a rote, calculated path. It is an explosive, messy, terrifying, and passionate adventure.

How can your work take you on a journey?

What dragons are to be slayed?

What myths are to be broken?

What music is meant to be danced to, until there is no separation between beat, body, and spirit?

Which battles are to be fought?

What deep, passionate love is to be made?

What inner tiger is meant to be released from its chains?

How would you feel differently about your craft if you viewed it as a noble adventure?

One of the great burdens of creative people is wondering, after looking at what they have done: "Is this all just a bunch of meaningless drivel? Do I have any idea what I am doing?"

It is also the great burden of experienced creatives.

As a little girl, I sat in the darkroom with my dad as he showed me subtle manipulations to the printing of photographs that made a huge difference in the feeling and look of the picture. I watched him smile as he found the one shot in eighty that captured just the right collection of facial expressions in a group shot.

To my dad, a craft is a noble undertaking. He takes his

photography seriously. And his writing. And his work restoring the Port Costa School.

Even in the last quarter of your life, you can never consider yourself a master at the end of the journey.

Choose adventure.

When you choose the adventure of your craft, you find unexpected, beautiful, and unlikely twists and turns that you never expected.

Differentiation, as the marketing wonks like to say.

Are you on an adventure?

Who is the hero?

Who are you trying to save?

How would your work be different if you didn't have to sound pithy or appear perfect?

Part two: Develop a mastery mind-set

Your body of work will broaden and deepen over time. Its value is determined by your commitment to continually improve your skills and deepen your ingredients.

When you focus on mastering your chosen craft, many opportunities open up for you.

In today's world of hacks, shortcuts, and instant money-making blueprints, I think we have lost appreciation for slow-brewing mastery in our work.

Through the years, I have worked with many martial artists, cultural leaders, and business mentors who have taught me that trying to finish first in a short race is not only stressful, it also works against developing deep expertise.

Here are eleven ways to develop a mastery mind-set.

1. Learn patience

My mother-in-law has taught me that Diné people (Navajos) have ceremonies for every part of life. There are ceremonies at a baby's first laugh, at puberty, and for the changing seasons. There are water ceremonies and lightning ceremonies and blessing ceremonies. In these sacred gatherings, conversation is slow and deliberate and unhurried. An elder can take an entire hour to share a teaching, or to bless a meal. I have watched elders see a young person squirm with impatience, then choose to talk slower and longer. They do this because they know that learning to settle down and develop patience is going to help the young develop thoughtfulness, depth, and wisdom.

2. Practice the basics

When we first learn a new skill, we dive into it with abandon, taking classes, learning from mentors, and practicing like crazy. When we reach a certain level of success, we often get lazy. True masters never stop practicing the basics. Martial artists do push-ups and sit-ups every day of their lives. Artists practice brush strokes. Writers write daily. Entrepreneurs create, market, and sell. When you don't practice the basics, *they go away.*

3. Appreciate the source of your materials

In a film called *Jiro Dreams of Sushi*, Jiro's son walks slowly around the fish market, looking for the perfect fish for the evening meals. He has relationships with fishermen who will not sell their product to anyone but him. Great work is built with great materials, by people and partners who care as much about what they do as you care about what you do. Avoid cheap, sloppy, and poorly constructed tools and materials.

4. Deconstruct everything

Often success is random. If you started a business in 1996 like I did, you might have thought you were naturally talented. The market was flourishing. Companies were throwing huge sums of money around for training, employee perks, and expensive toys. If you do well, take the time to figure out exactly which conditions led to your success. If you have a raging failure, figure out exactly which conditions, personal and environmental, led to your downfall.

5. Set boundaries

You cannot create great work if you are in a constant state of defense. You must protect your creative work time by blocking out your schedule, turning off your phone, and closing down your e-mail. You must protect your creative energy by avoiding "life-sucking squids," as my friend Martha Beck calls people who care only about their own edification and not about your needs or soul.

6. Make your space holy

When you respect your work, you want to create a beautiful, clean, sacred container for it. Regardless of the size, cost, or fanciness of your physical space, treat it with reverence. Pay attention to what you bring into it. Take time to clean the floor and wash the windows. Surround yourself with images of beauty and inspiration. Give gratitude to the tools that you use to do your work and to all the masters who have come before you.

7. Cultivate your voice

While you can become fluent in another language, you will never feel more anchored and at home than when you are speaking your native tongue. Explore your voice. Listen to your intuition. Write down your thoughts. Develop your ideas. Don't get distracted by your love for someone else's voice, which will only lead to cheap knockoffs.

8. Swallow your pride

True mastery is based on a love affair with your work. You want to take a great photograph, or write a great paragraph, or lead a transformational coaching call because you want to make the *profession* proud. You want to please the past masters and the art itself. If your work is criticized, or isn't up to your own standards, don't take it personally. If you receive lots of accolades and exposure, don't let it get to your head. Keep your focus on honoring your profession.

9. Punch through the bag

My mixed martial arts teacher, Kelly Fiori, always tells me to "punch through the bag" when I am practicing jabs and crosses. If you just focus on hitting the target itself, your punch will be weak. Set your target a foot behind the bag, and aim to hit that. The same applies to your work. How does today's goal relate to tomorrow's goal, and next year's goal? How will your choices today affect your relatives in seven generations? Always think ahead.

10. When imitated, don't retaliate, innovate

When you are great at what you do, people are bound to imitate you. Sometimes they will try to steal your intellectual property, or students, or employees, or business model, or artistic genre. It is natural to get upset when this happens. But instead of fighting with the imitator, move on to innovate the next stage of your work. If you are doing your job well, your work is constantly improving and growing. Imitate *that*.

Once you begin to cultivate a mastery mind-set, life slows down and you appreciate the delicious nuances in every moment. And when you sink into that way of living, you may begin to realize that mastery is not even the end goal.

11. Think like a scientist
There's one more critical step in developing a mastery mind-set: learning how to not take failure, or success, personally. You must learn to get comfortable with putting your work in the world and evaluating all feedback from an objective perspective.

In my work as a business coach, I am frequently asked to explain the key ingredient to becoming a successful entrepreneur. Is it a great idea? Financial backing? A charismatic founder? A bulletproof business plan? Great selling skills?

These can certainly help. But what will make or break your entrepreneurial journey is: the ability to think like a scientist.

What I mean specifically is a willingness to create a working hypothesis, test it, observe with curiosity, ask why, tweak, retest, observe, et cetera, until you are satisfied.

When you view building your body of work as a series of experiments, it is interesting, intellectually stimulating, and similar to solving a puzzle.

In contrast, when you view your creative process or journey as an epic Hollywood drama of sweeping success or crushing failure, chances are you will not last very long and will be an emotional wreck by the end.

Few people are as enthusiastic, and relentless, about testing as my friend Ramit Sethi. In a blog post, he lays out numerous examples of the power of testing your assumptions. My favorite is the best man who spent seven months perfecting a wedding toast.

Now, that is a friend you want to have.

Brian Clark of Copyblogger shares the same enthusiasm for testing when examining Web page conversion.

Who would have known that given a choice, more people would click a button that says IT'S FREE rather than SIGN UP FREE or FREE SIGN-UP. Or that changing a sign-up button color from green to red would boost conversion by 21 percent? Brian has built a thriving business, sharing tips on tiny twists and tweaks that add up to successful online commerce.

So if you find yourself thinking, "I *knew* I should never have approached that store with an offer to sell my spicy almonds, they *rejected* me!" put on your scientist hat and think instead, "How fascinating! I thought the store would be excited about selling my spicy almonds, but they were not. I wonder why."

Part three: Scope, test, scope, test

When you set big goals, it is easy to get overwhelmed with the enormity of the task at hand. A critical part of the creative process is continually breaking down the work into manageable chunks.

Use these steps when testing your projects.

1. Look for models

The first place I send clients who are trying to do something totally new is in search of business models that are already working.

If you are a world-class tuba teacher and have always delivered your lessons in person but want to deliver all your lessons over Skype, look for evidence of someone who has used a similar tool for educational purposes. If you find a tutorial that contains technical information but not much about the business model, you may want to dig further and find music teachers who sell virtual music lessons successfully. Or you might find someone in a related subject area, like an art teacher, who sells e-books and video training programs to supplement live art lessons.

The key is to find someone who is doing business in an innovative *and* effective way, and to pull back the curtain so that you understand the key parts of their business model. (If you want to get lots of ideas for business models, you will love the *Business Model Generation* handbook).

2. Define the phases

You may not know every last thing about building a business, but with some input from experienced colleagues or business mentors and your business model research, you should be able to define the overall phases you need to go through to reach your goal.

One time, a LaidOffCamp participant I spoke to at an event wanted to create a mixture of live classes and high-quality information products for her art business. I recommended that she:

- define the target market.
- identify the key desires, problems, or challenges in her area of expertise.
- create an initial offering of a product or service that solves the target market's problem.
- test the offering with a set number of ideal participants (at this stage, she can choose not to charge for it).
- debrief the test and determine how it could be replicated.
- identify partners with access to the ideal target market.
- develop more offerings, perhaps with partners, and test again.
- flesh out the business plan with lessons learned, identifying a ripe offering that can grow.
- accelerate the marketing machine, which includes building a mailing list, utilizing social media and PR effectively, and participating in live events.
- develop an online product to sell to the market when the list grows.
- test, debrief, and continue building products and services.

These steps may change based on your specific goals and objectives, but at least you can get clear as to what to build, in what order.

3. Choose a specific small test related to the big goal, and define the desired outcome

Once you have a sense of the major phases involved in reaching your big goal, you want to quickly look for a small test that will bring you into the real world, with real customers.

Time and time again, I see new entrepreneurs get stuck in the planning stage and think things have to be perfect in order to bring them to market. This will kill both your momentum and your spirit. To nip this momentum killer in the bud, choose one small activity that will get you moving in the real world. It should be:

- Short—Never do your first test for a six-week program. Start with an hour-long class.

- Relatively easy—If you need subjects to test your program, tap into people who already know, like, and trust you. There is a reason chefs test their recipes on their own family first!

Testing will give you two kinds of data.

- Enjoyment factor—How does it feel to do the "thing" that you have been aching to do? If you have always wanted to be a coach, how does it actually feel to coach? If you have never done it before, it is normal to have a bit of anxiety, but it should still feel like you are moving in the right direction. (Martha Beck uses a quick assessment— does it feel "shackles on" or "shackles off" when you think about or do something?) Terror is often involved when doing new things, but it can still taste and feel like freedom.

- Reality factor—How easy or difficult was it to execute this small test? Did things turn out as planned? What did you learn from the experience that you will apply to future tests?

Once you define the test, then define specific elements to measure, such as:

- How many calls or e-mails did it take to fill the event?
- Which marketing strategies worked? (Facebook, flier in coffee shops, Twitter, e-mail, et cetera.)
- How much time was involved in preparation?
- How much did materials cost?
- How did the test participants react? (*Always* get feedback after a test! If you are live with people, you could get a video testimonial on your phone, pass out written evaluation forms, or follow up with an e-mail survey.)
- How did it feel? Why was it so fantastic, or so terrible?

4. Execute your small test

When you get one very specific task to test, give it your full attention. Don't worry about the bigger goals at this point, since they will just distract you.

You will move quickly when you choose a specific date to execute the test. So choose your date, identify your test subjects, and go do the thing. It may not be ideal. It won't be perfect. But it's one step forward.

5. Review results

I mentioned before how important it is to be a scientist in your entrepreneurial journey. Since you have defined your metrics from the outset, it will not be hard to measure your results versus your plan.

Once you review the results, ask yourself:

- What would I do differently next time?
- How could I streamline the steps involved in this activity?
- Is this scalable?
- If so, who are other people or where are other markets who might be interested in this?
- Do I want to continue doing it?

When you get in the practice of executing small tests of the pieces of your body of work, real progress happens.

A test coaching session can lead to a three-month coaching service, which leads to a busy blog and a robust mix of digital courses, live retreats, two books, and speaking engagements. I should know, that's how I started.

Testing recipes at a law office (while still a lawyer) can lead to custom cake orders, seven retail stores, three cookbooks, and an appearance on *Oprah*. Just ask Warren Brown, founder of CakeLove.

Experimenting with graphic design services may lead to software application development, which leads to a family of applications, a bestselling book, a killer blog, and juicy speaking engagements. Just ask the founders of 37signals.

And creating a music video for an unknown rapper led

Kanye West to hire the Mikes to tour the world with him for two years.

The process of scoping and testing continues throughout the development of your project. If you are paying attention to the results, you may end up with a different final project than you originally intended. This is fine. What really matters is that you create something you are proud of that becomes a powerful addition to your body of work.

Part four: Flex your creative muscles

Technique, speed, power

In my mixed martial arts class, my instructor, Kelly, told us exactly how we should train our kickboxing combinations.

"First, focus on technique. Do the movements very slowly so that you get a good feel for the correct movements.

"Then, when you feel confident in the technique, add speed. Do the movements quicker.

"Finally, add power. Pay attention to the force that comes through your body, and direct it to your target.

"The technique, speed, and power together is what will make you a great fighter."

This is where we get stuck in the creative process.

When doing an activity for the first time, like writing a sales page, we have the expectation that we will get power (conversion) and speed (lots of buyers) from the initial technique.

In reality, the very first time you do it is a big accomplishment in itself. It's a victory just to get a mediocre sales page live on the Web.

As you go through time, you improve your page by focusing on power activities—practicing persuasive writing, making clearer offers, working on fresh design, and creating compelling testimonials.

And the more you work on this, the more your speed picks up. More people buy and spread the word about your great product, which attracts more people to the page and feeds the speed of sale.

When a student in my power teaching class taught her first class, she said, "It was exhausting! I wrote a ten-page script for the first class to make sure I covered everything. When you teach a class, you make it seem so easy!"

I replied, "That is because I have taught more than one hundred classes."

I have repeatedly worked on the technique of designing a class, have honed my power by zeroing in on specific teaching and speaking methodologies, and I have taught thousands of people. But if I had not started with my first awkward and painful class, I would never have gotten to a place of ease and comfort.

We abandon our efforts too early

There is so much focus on quick, easy marketing techniques that we forget that true, deep, authentic, meaningful, and lasting business competence comes from technique, speed, and power training.

In my recent survey to blog readers and clients, the majority of the five hundred respondents said their business goals for 2013 were to improve their marketing and sales competency. This will work only if they stop trying individual marketing techniques once, then abandoning them for the next shiny marketing-technique du jour.

Your challenge

Choose an important creative activity you completed in the last thirty days.

Step 1: Identify how well you executed the technique the first time.

Step 2: Identify the power activities that will increase your competency and improve your results the next time.

Step 3: Invest in your power activities. Get expert input. Re-write clunky areas. Get feedback from your target audience. Read books. Watch videos. Look at case studies of successful examples.

Step 4: Do the creative activity again.

Repeat steps 2, 3 and 4.

Do the creative activity again.

Repeat steps 2, 3 and 4.

Repeat the entire process for the next year.

Send me a big check, because I know you will be *smashing* your professional results at the end of the year.

The 20X Rule

Much of my time spent coaching is egging my clients on so they finish their websites, pitch new clients, and test and try new products in the market.

The enemy of a new entrepreneur is endless planning and perfection.

After celebrating that they finally took a serious first step, I often get a slightly dejected e-mail or deflated check-in on the next coaching call.

"I sent that e-mail to two potential clients, but neither of them has gotten back to me yet."

"I designed and launched the teleclass we talked about, but only one person signed up. And it was my sister."

It is at this moment that I have to explain the 20X Rule.

In business, as well as in other areas of life, you have to sow twenty times more seeds than you think is realistic or necessary to make things happen.

You will set yourself up for heartbreak and mediocrity if you don't radically adjust your expectations for the amount of outreach and connections it takes to do creative work.

What do you think would happen over the course of one year if:

- Instead of reaching out to one new journalist a month, you reached out to twenty?
- Instead of reaching two prospective clients a month, you reached forty?
- Instead of testing three new product ideas a year, you tested sixty?

Chances are you would see some radically different results.

When I first started my newsletter eight years ago, it took me two months to write one article.

Now I crack out twenty times the content in one month and don't even break a sweat.

If you get results sooner, great.

Maybe you will have fantastic luck and with some strategic thinking will reach out to three qualified clients and book your business.

I would rather you expect to reach out to sixty and be happy it took fewer contacts than be crushed that you don't sign up your first client the first time you reach out to them.

Building your body of work is a marathon. Train for it.

Creating will save us

The night before the Grammys in 2012, host LL Cool J was interviewed by Piers Morgan on CNN.

The interview covered a lot of ground, including how LL Cool J (born James Todd Smith) came out of a very tough childhood and created a solid family base and lots of commercial and financial success. He credits his grandmother for orienting him toward the future by repeatedly quoting, "If a task is once begun, never leave it till it's done. Be thy labor great or small, do it well or not at all."

Piers asked him what we needed to do as a country to "keep America great."

His answer made me sit up in my chair.

"I think in order to keep America great, we have to keep America creative."

I think he hit it on the head.

We love to argue. To point fingers. To debate.

That will not solve our economic problems, nor make us feel powerful.

We are made to create. We feel useful when we create. We release our "stuckness" when we create. We reinvent our lives, tell new stories, and rebuild communities when we create. We reclaim our esteem, our muse, and our hope when we create.

It is why your particular work mode does not matter. If you are creating something of value and personal meaning, does it really matter if you are self-employed, freelancing, or employed by a corporation or nonprofit?

The act of creating is what sets us free, what gives our life meaning. And it is what will put us back on our personal and collective path to greatness.

Exercise: Pocket Planner

The new world of work is a series of creative projects. What is the next thing you want to add to your body of work? Use this planner to sketch it out, and get busy creating!

What do you want to create?
Name it. Describe it.

(A book, a job, a video, an app)

Who is it for?
Describe your audience.

(Specific details about who they are)

Why does it need to get done?
Describe the roots of the project.

(How does this fit in your body of work? Who will be affected by it? What good thing will happen as the result of you completing it?)

How are you going to structure the project?
Define a model.

(Who has done something like this before? How was it structured? How can you customize this model and make it your own?)

When does it need to be done?

Set a deadline.

(Nothing happens without a deadline. Set a date, and work your project plan backward.)

Next: Create a prototype so you can test the idea in the easiest and quickest way possible, with the fewest amount of resources.

CHAPTER 6

Surf the Fear

> Pain can be almost impossible to bear, but suffering is even more difficult. When you refuse to accept pain, you will suffer. When you cling to getting what you want and refuse to accept what you have, you will suffer. Fighting reality, opposing the inevitable, or struggling against what is—causes suffering.
>
> —Dr. Brent Menninger

Rafe Eric Biggs was a leadership coach in the San Francisco Bay Area, with a PhD in organizational psychology. He worked with managers and teams in Silicon Valley. He was handsome and athletic, with an active social life.

Always interested in expanding his training and certifications, Rafe got a coaching degree in somatic education, a body-centered approach to personal development. "I was integrating the work in my coaching, and then I felt a deeper calling to study more about transformation and healing."

At the same time, the economy was slowing down, and Rafe decided to take a break from work to travel internationally for an extended period. His girlfriend at the time was a massage therapist and wanted to go to Thailand to study Thai massage. So they packed up their house, put everything in storage, and took off on an adventure.

For four months, he lived in Thailand, studying massage and enjoying the slow pace and relaxed lifestyle. His girlfriend went back to the United States, and they eventually decided to take a break from dating.

"I was probably paying, like, seven dollars a night for a beach bungalow, and I was living so inexpensively," Rafe said. "I was able to learn about shamanic healing and take yoga workshops, [attend] meditation retreats, and meet some really amazing people. So I was kind of inspired by that and just really enjoying being in the moment and just choosing to do whatever I wanted to do. It was such freedom. After four months, I wanted to go somewhere else. And I was going to go to Bali because I wanted to study more about shamanism and spirituality. Then a friend of mine said, 'Well, if you really want to learn about spirituality, you should go to India.' I had a little bit of fear about going there because I heard about people getting really sick. But when my friend said, 'You should go to India,' there was a voice inside me that said very clearly, 'Go to India.' I accepted that that is where I was supposed to go."

Rafe flew to New Delhi and was overwhelmed by the amount of people and stimulation. So he headed to Dharamshala, near the Dalai Lama's home, and decided to do a ten-day silent meditation retreat.

"I was able to really confront a lot of my own fears about

myself, and I was able to get to a place of stillness and clarity about what I wanted to do next in my life. What I realized was that I really wanted to live more in a community with other like-minded people and I wanted to find a way to live a much more simple life without having to work so hard."

At the end of the retreat, Rafe and his friends had a celebratory dinner on a patio rooftop of a guesthouse. After dinner, people started dancing, and he noticed that there was no guardrail around the perimeter of the roof. He saw a candle and picked it up to go set it by the edge.

"As I walked towards the edge of the roof, the candle light just blinded me for a split second and I stepped off and I fell about ten or twelve feet. The next thing I know, I'm laying on my back, looking at the stars, and I was like, 'Wow. How did I get here?' So I tried to sit up and I couldn't. I was like, 'Oh crap, something's wrong.' But you know, I wasn't really in a state of fear. I think it was from all the meditation I did. I said, 'Everything's fine. I'm going to be okay.'"

After being rushed to the hospital and having surgery, Rafe woke up and was told he was paralyzed from the chest down. He suddenly had to face life as a quadriplegic.

Fear is inevitable

One of the most wonderful, and terrifying, things about life is that we have no idea how it is going to turn out.

We get sick or injured. People we love die. The economy crashes. Spouses leave. A business partner runs away with our money. We take a big risk to be creative in our presentation and fail miserably, in public.

Because the new world of work is unstable and unpredictable, uncertainty, fear, and doubt are inevitable parts of building your body of work.

Managing fear and uncertainty is core to thriving and surviving in this environment.

Rafe said, "I believe that my calling going to India was to have a spiritual awakening, and that happened. It just wasn't the way I thought it was going to happen."

Most of us cannot imagine having such an enlightened attitude about life after experiencing such a devastating setback. But Rafe leaned on the skills he had developed in the years he had been an organizational consultant and coach, especially his somatic coaching.

While it is normal for people to get depressed or afraid about the unknown, the key is to keep moving forward by focusing on the future. If you focus on what you want in your life instead of what you don't want, you'll see your opportunities expand.

In order to develop resilience in the face of fear and uncertainty like Rafe, you need four skills.

Skill 1: View adversity as a means of growth
Skill 2: Diagnose your fear
Skill 3: Process the unexpected
Skill 4: Overcome distress and procrastination

Skill 1: View adversity as a means of growth

In the startup world, we love to tell stories of how the most successful people faced adversity. We hear about the catastrophic product launches, bankruptcy, divorce, and health scares—all part of the hero's journey to becoming a wealthy, successful businessperson.

A typical entrepreneur success formula

Register business name.
Launch website.
Try to sell something.
Have massive humiliating failure.
Make a change.
Have massive success.
Hire one thousand employees.
Write a book describing said humiliating failure followed
    by massive success.
Plan speaking tour and tell humiliating failure story, fol-
    lowed by dramatic business success story.
Appear on cover of *Inc.* magazine in confident pose.
Tell failure and success story on the *Today* show.
Sell your company to Google.
Repeat.

Such success is actually very rare, but failure is always an essential part of the story.

So if failure is such a key element of business lore, why do we get upset when it happens to us? It's because we think that our *particular* humiliating failure is much greater than the failures of those we admire.

Sure, Richard Branson says, "There are many ways to run a successful company. What works once may never work again. What everyone tells you never to do may just work, once. There are no rules. You don't learn to walk by follow-ing rules. You learn by doing, and by falling over, and it's because you fall over that you learn to save yourself from falling over."

But inside you say, "Surely Richard Branson has never really struggled, or if he did, it was over something as minuscule as a typo. I am sure he felt absolutely confident in his ability to become a billionaire business person. He is Richard Branson, after all."

My take?

Richard Branson felt the same humiliation and fear when failing that you may be feeling about some aspect of your life at this moment. He just got up and kept going. And he chose not to turn his failure into shame.

Checklist

No matter the severity of the challenge you are facing, ask yourself these questions:

This experience is:

- ❏ preparing me to do great work.

- ❏ preparing me to be a smarter, kinder, or more compassionate person.

- ❏ teaching me exactly what I need to know so I can create better, more effective work.

- ❏ reminding me of what my true, natural strengths are and aren't.

- ❏ pushing me to make an urgent decision about something that is critical to my well-being.

❏   teaching me what I need to get help with, outsource,
    or stop doing.

❏   teaching me to have more patience.

❏   fulfilling my destiny.

After his accident and physical therapy, Rafe became interested in dating again but faced the challenge of navigating a
new world of sexuality after disability.

"There are a lot of people I notice with disabilities, including myself, who feel like that part of their life feels kind of cut
off, and so they have to figure out new ways to be intimate with
their partners. That's when I started really exploring sexuality
and disability and started doing research."

Rafe now coaches individuals and couples who are navigating sexuality and disability, and is developing online courses
with a partner to serve this market.

By establishing new roots of meaning, and finding purpose in finding answers to his own questions, he is expanding
and deepening his own body of work.

When I first heard the news of Rafe's accident, I worried
what his life would be like. Now, I am inspired by his story and
use it to motivate myself when I get scared, overwhelmed, or
frustrated.

If Amanda Wang (from chapter 2) and Rafe can learn to
lead positive lives of great contribution, and continue to build
impressive bodies of work despite serious mental and physical
restrictions, so can you.

Frame your adversity as a temporary setback and keep
building your body of work.

Skill 2: Diagnose your fear

Your fear shares critical information with you multiple times a day. We are often encouraged to "crush the fear," "ignore the fear," or "stomp on fear."

I prefer to surf the fear.

Author and coach Martha Beck describes the part of our brain that generates a lot of ongoing fear in her book *Steering by Starlight*.

> One of the deepest layers of your brain is a neural structure that first evolved in early vertebrates—specifically, reptiles. Because of this, scientists call it the reptilian brain. It's wrapped around your brain stem, deep in the center of your head, like the serpent twined around the knowledge tree in the Garden of Eden. . . . The entire purpose of your reptilian brain is to continuously broadcast survival fears—alarm reactions that keep animals alive in the wild. These fears fall into two categories: lack and attack. On one hand, our reptilian brains are convinced that we lack everything we need: We don't have enough love, time, money, *everything*. On the other hand, something terrible is about to happen. A predator—human or animal—is poised to snatch us!

The protective instinct of your lizard brain can help you develop tremendous awareness and a healthy, motivated attitude toward your success.

When you are gripped by fear, you need to slow down and process the emotion in the rational part of your brain.

Try to talk through your fears with a compassionate person. If that's not possible, write down the answers to these questions:

- What are you afraid of?
- Why are you afraid of it?
- What do you need to know to reduce the fear?
- If you were to practice this thing that you are afraid of doing, would it get better?
- Is this thing you are afraid of something that is negative or unhealthy for you, or a positive opportunity for growth?
- If this is a positive opportunity for growth, who do you know who might be able to help you overcome your fear?

Full-color, full-contact living

The first-time advice about defense in mixed martial arts seems crazy.

A large-fisted person is coming toward you with a side hook, and you are advised to cover the side of your face with your arm and *lean in to* the blow.

It makes a lot of sense when you think about it. When your face is protected, leaning into the oncoming punch breaks the speed of the movement with all of your body weight. As soon as you defend and stop the punch, you are in perfect range to launch an uppercut to your opponent's jaw.

But while your mind understands that it makes sense, every bit of your instinct tells you to run like hell.

The same thing happens when fear, discomfort, uncertainty, or doubt slips into our lives.

Whether we are making a positive change that invokes fear (going for a promotion, waiting to hear about a book deal, speaking in front of a large audience for the first time), the instinct is to avoid fear and anxiety.

Our best defense in life is to lean into the fear. Feel the emotion. Take a blow or two in order to really learn what you need to protect.

As Kelly Fiori tells me if I tense up during a self-defense practice, "Relax! Take a second to assess your situation, then you can react with your muscle memory."

The $4,000 thought

In 2012, I was on a coaching call with Antrese Wood, an artist client who had a significant goal to raise $25,000 on Kickstarter so she could travel to all the provinces of Argentina and paint the people and places that defined the country. She had raised $8,400 so far, with twelve days to go for her thirty-day campaign and was frustrated with the stalled momentum. Too shy to reach out to people who had already supported the project, she said, "I don't want to bug the people who have donated to the project with updates about what I am doing. It is my job to make this happen."

I immediately saw that this attitude was causing stalled momentum, not a lack of interest from supporters.

"What if you thought about it differently?" I said. "What if you thought, 'People who have signed up to support the project are excited to see it succeed. If I ask for help, I am opening an opportunity for them to get more involved in the project and more excited.'"

She changed her thought, sent a project update to current supporters, and twenty-four hours later, her project had raised $4,000 more toward her goal.

The only difference between an idea and a concrete, live piece of your body of work is the thought that triggers your action.

Your thoughts, beliefs, and assumptions drive everything in your life and career.

People who operate on a high level of creativity and mastery are rigorous about mental awareness and preparation. Top athletes, fighters, artists, writers, businesspeople, and scientists use different methods to stay clear, focused, motivated, and productive.

Not only are precise and motivating thoughts critical to maintaining momentum toward big goals, but the ability to look at things from new and critical perspectives is a fundamental skill in creating a diverse, interesting, and integrated body of work.

WHAT TO DO WHEN YOU ARE DOING EVERY-THING RIGHT AND NOTHING IS HAPPENING

Renita Kalhorn is a peak-performance coach and Juilliard-trained classical pianist and has an MBA and black belt in taekwon-do. She mentors Navy SEAL candidates in mental toughness and counts NASA and Fortune 500 CEOs among her clients.

She suggests this exercise when you feel like you aren't making any progress in your projects:

If you can't change your circumstances, you need to change the way you *think* about the circumstances.

Grab a pen and piece of paper. This three-step "perspective reset" will take less than twenty minutes and is guaranteed to rekindle motivation (do it alone or as a team).

1. Make a "Things I've (We've) Done" list.

As a species, humans are predisposed to notice the negative. No matter where we are in life, we tend to focus on how long it's taking to get "over there" and where we want to go—totally discounting how far we've come.

So Step 1 is to acknowledge what you've done: the clients you do have, the development progress you have made, the sales/traffic you have accumulated. This helps you regain your equilibrium and reaffirm that you haven't been doing nothing.

2. Make a "Things I (We) Haven't Tried Yet" list.

Even though it may feel like you've done absolutely everything possible, there are inevitably new angles you haven't explored and people you haven't contacted. Making a list of these can actually be encouraging because it helps you see that there are still things that you can do to impact your results.

Then, rather than trying to do them all, choose one that has the highest potential impact.

3. Expand your idea of what's possible.

It's easy to look at other people's success and think it was a smooth ride. Not surprisingly, comparing ourselves with others when we're already feeling inadequate spirals down into negativity and feeling like "it's never gonna happen."

The way to nip this in the bud is to cultivate possibility thinking—to go beyond the current reality and stretch your belief of what's possible. Jump on Google or YouTube and actively look for examples where people achieved success in the face of great odds or made a serendipitous out-of-nowhere connection.

Immerse your mind with stories and references on a regular basis and they will become the new normal.

Skill 3: Process the unexpected

About five years into the Port Costa School restoration project, after countless weeks of back-breaking cleanup work, a huge rainfall caused a large tree to block a drainage pipe that flowed under the school. The entire basement was flooded, destroying years of work and tens of thousands of dollars' worth of materials and labor.

My dad and stepmom Diane and the community of volunteers were devastated. After dealing with the immediate cleanup, they were faced with a difficult question: Is it worth it to go on?

Diane went to work researching alternatives and found out that the Federal Emergency Management Association (FEMA) might be able to cover some of the damage. So she wrote an incredibly long application and patiently worked the process for a couple of years. FEMA was able to cover the cost of rerouting the pipe under the school (to avoid future floods) and repouring the concrete for the foundation.

By being creative and flexible, they were able to recover from an unexpected natural disaster and continue to rebuild the Port Costa School.

When something very difficult happens to you, process it through these four steps.

1. Fall apart

Getting injured, getting laid off, losing face, or losing those you love will immobilize you in the short term. When difficult things happen, feel them. Cry. Hug someone. Grieve. It is perfectly natural to not want to get right back to business when terrible things happen. Express the emotion in a safe setting.

2. Honor what you have

When something bad happens, it is easy to get stuck grieving everything you have lost. While this step is extremely important, once you have grieved, you need to remind yourself of the good things you still have in your life. If you lost your job, do you still have a loving relationship with your spouse? If you experience a health setback, do you appreciate the generosity of your friends and family as they nurse you back to health?

Sometimes it takes losing big things to realize the value of small things in our life.

3. Never forget, but choose to create a new future

While in the midst of a huge, painful challenge, it is impossible to imagine a new future. You want to slug anyone who suggests that "everything happens for a reason." Yet over and over again, I have seen people rise from huge heartbreak and build a new life. My client Sarah has been working on an amazing fair-trade project with Rwandan artisans called Songa Designs. If you know anything about Rwandan history in the 1990s, you know that it is filled with unimaginable terror and genocide. Yet tremendous beauty exists in the art and economy being built by Rwandan people today.

We can learn from those who have witnessed the worst of humanity and still choose to build the best for humanity.

4. Be supported, and support others

My husband's older brother was killed when he was eighteen. When I have talked about it with his mom, mixed with tears and pain, she always tells stories about the people who were so strong for her and held her closely when she was overcome with grief. And I have seen her be strong for others who have experienced their own losses. We never know when we will be the one who does not have the strength to go on and needs to surrender to the arms of our loved ones and community members. There is no shame in surrendering, and there is great valor in holding others in times of unbearable grief.

I sincerely hope that challenge or tragedy does not visit you or your family. But if it does, know that you are not alone. Others have experienced a similar challenge and have found a way to create a new normal worth living.

Skill 4: Deal with procrastination and distress

I always know right before I am about to slip into hell.

The day starts out innocently enough.

I brew a strong cup of Peet's French Roast. Then I walk outside barefoot to the backyard and sit down to listen to the birds and to smell the fresh air and to see the bright sun peeking up from behind the Superstition Mountains. The stillness of the morning makes everything feel fresh and new.

As the coffee kicks in, I think about the work I need to get done that day.

I may need to write a part of my new book. Or course materials for a class I am teaching. Or a sales letter for a new product.

There are always little things to do, like guest posts or book blurbs.

The list feels feasible. The day stretches out in front of me like a slow summer day. Peaceful, open, expansive.

After dropping off the kids, I get into the office and settle in.

I check e-mail, open HootSuite, and look at my Twitter stream. It feels good to connect with my community and catch up on the prior night's missed replies.

The hour starts to slip away.

I want to get started on my to-do list, but I know that I still have plenty of time. So I keep surfing around and get a little inspiration.

A TED talk might fire me up, so I watch my favorite.

Feeling good, I open Scrivener and start writing.

But before I get more than a few words on the page, I realize that I never got back to someone interested in hiring me to speak.

So I switch over to e-mail and find and respond to the inquiry.

More e-mails have come in, so I take care of the urgent ones for a few minutes.

A coaching call is coming up in about forty-five minutes, so I realize I don't have enough time to really get on a roll and finish a project.

And I start to feel slightly sick inside.

Trying to shake it off, I busy myself with a bit of administrative work, none of which is on my critical and important list.

The coaching call comes and goes.

I call my best friend and get inspired talking about a new future project.

It is now about one forty-five.

I suddenly feel the pressure of the end of the day coming.

No longer an open, expansive stretch of time, the day has turned into a vise, and it begins squeezing my head.

I start to feel desperate.

Like a moth drawn to a camping lantern, I am pulled into a new tab of the endless Internet.

It leads to more videos and news stories.

I turn to Twitter to drum up some conversation. I want to feel better.

And I think, "This day is gone. I am gone, and I didn't get a damned thing done."

I have been defeated by what Steven Pressfield calls Resistance. The insidious, sulphur-scented dragon of a beast whose sole intention is to suck all the intelligence, creativity, and goodness out of my body and heart.

All that is left is a defeated shadow of my real self, with a stomachache and sugar hangover. Longing to go to sleep to start the day over again tomorrow.

Resistance is fierce, and there are days when it kicks my ass.

It doesn't have to.

Productivity hacks among you could identify dozens of critical flaws in the way I start my day. You are probably right.

We all need to study the beast and adjust our creative process so that we do not experience lost days.

Do you ever have those moments?

Amid the frantic rush between breakfast, school drop-offs, calls, e-mails, and deadlines, or after a stretch of mindless television or Internet surfing, you suddenly realize that time is slipping by. You might say to yourself: "This is how I am choosing to spend my time. My creativity, and the great ideas that are supposed to change my life, are slowly withering, along with my brain cells. Is this really how I want to spend my life?"

What do you do when you are confronted with the realization that your life is finite? And that the way you are spending today really matters in the big scheme of things?

You can choose to panic. Or, you can choose to be grateful for the lesson.

And you can change.

If you are not motivated to do something, try reminding yourself why it is important.

What is at the root of the task at hand? Why will doing it benefit you, those you care about, and the world at large? How will this help you reach longer-term goals that are important to you?

If you are not making progress, try changing up your pattern.

I always know when I am going through a significant growth stage because I revert to mind-numbing activities to quell the fear. I read *People* magazine, spend too much time sharing motivational quotes on Facebook, or watch really bad television. When the pattern starts to drag on for a few days, it is important to change up your habits.

Find a new way to approach a scary task. Break it into tiny little bits. Work from a totally different location. Ask someone to talk you through an idea so you gain a new perspective and get out of your own head. Go for a walk. Draw a picture of the solution, instead of trying to write about it. Dance wildly to AC/DC or Jay Z instead of listening to your favorite classical music. Anything that will stop the unproductive pattern from repeating.

If you don't feel joy in the goals you have set for yourself, try changing your goals.

Are you tired of striving for accolades, promotions, or respect in your field? Do you pour yourself into each endeavor with great focus, only to feel kind of hollow when you succeed? Do you chair every PTA committee, go to Lego-building marathons with your kids, bake your own gluten-free bread, and still feel like a crappy parent?

Maybe you need to go chase fireflies.
Blackfoot warrior and orator Crowfoot said, "What is life? It is the flash of fireflies in the night. It is the breath of a buffalo in the wintertime. It is the little shadow that runs across the grass and loses itself in the sunset."

If you are waiting for the perfect time to lose weight, write a book, start a business, or find a mate, try starting now.
It will never be the perfect time to do anything. Take tiny steps in a new direction. Stop eating doughnuts for breakfast, and eat cereal instead. Create a Word document with the chapter headings, and write one paragraph of foolish nonsense. Put up a really ugly sales page with a two-paragraph description of your service and a PayPal button. Go on a Sierra Club hike.

If you are desperately searching for the answer to one question and not finding it, try asking another question.

"What is my passion?" or "What business should I start?" create despair in the hearts of many people. Try asking, "What am I thoroughly grateful for today?" or "What can I count on to make me happy, regardless of what is going on in my life?" (My kids, my dogs, my Peet's coffee.)

There is no right answer. There is only the opportunity to be aware of the tremendous blessing we have to wake up each day, breathe fresh air, and watch a shadow dance across the grass until it is swallowed up by the sun.

Hallelujah anyway

Anne Lamott, author of *Bird by Bird,* dispensed this advice about getting over procrastination after years of listening to her writing students make excuses about why they couldn't make time to write every day:

> The answer is simple: you decide to. Then you push back your sleeves and start writing. . . . And it will be completely awful. . . . And to that, I say, Welcome. That's what it's like to be a writer. . . . At my church, we sing a gospel song called "Hallelujah Anyway." Everything's a mess, and you're going down the tubes financially, and gaining weight? Well, Hallelujah anyway.

If there is one thing I know for sure from the twenty-plus years I have been coaching both martial arts and business, it is that with the right motivation and drive, people can make astounding, unexpected, nearly miraculous change. So if you have been stuck in an unfulfilling career for years, if you have wanted to write a book but never get to it, if you want to stop smoking, get in shape, or repair your fractured relationship with your ex-husband so that you can both be better parents, please know that it is possible to change. You just have to develop ways to quickly shift your mind-set when you get stuck.

Flip on your winner switch

My mixed martial arts teacher, Kelly, said, "*Go!*" and four of us who were lying on our backs flipped over on our stomachs and dove for the two black training pads that were sitting in the center of the mat.

"Fight for it!" he yelled, as we wrestled each other for control.

I twisted and clutched a corner of the pad, trying to pull it away from my formidable opponent. She pinned me against the floor, and I felt my forehead break into a sweat as I shifted my hips to try and knock her off-balance so I could weaken her hold.

After one minute, we were getting tired, but we kept at it.

"Time!" he yelled.

My chest heaving, I gave my opponent a high five.

"Some of you are holding back in your training," said Master. "You need to realize that you are playing to win. When you are faced with a real-life situation when someone has your back on the ground, you will be fighting for your life. Are you going to fight halfway then?"

Then he said, "You have to learn to flip on your winner switch."

A lightbulb went on in my head.

So many people who are in the middle of a big creative project get racked with self-doubt about their ability to deliver the goods. This makes perfect sense—if you haven't done something before, you cannot be certain that you will do it well.

The only answer is to flip on your winner switch.

The winner switch is:

- focusing your complete attention and energy on the task at hand.
- recalling times when you have been successful in the past, and harnessing this positive state of mind.
- setting the intention to deliver killer results.
- doing your very best to complete the task, even when your face is being smashed into the ground and you are clearly outmatched.

Remember that the only way to get better is to train like a winner, getting expert feedback along the way. The more you train, the better you get, and the more you have winning results, the better you can surf the fear.

Exercise: How to Flip On Your Winner Switch

When you feel stuck or fearful, you need to learn quick ways to change your mood and regain your confidence. Follow these steps, and notice a dramatic change in your results.

1.   Create a "motivating music" playlist.
Choose music that gets you motivated. As a martial artist,
I am always inspired to get focused by *Rocky III*'s anthem
"Eye of the Tiger." You may enjoy heavy metal, hip-hop, or
relaxing music that gets you in the creative flow.

2.   Remove all distractions.
Turn off your phone, clean your desk, and disable social
media so you can totally focus on the task at hand.

3.   Describe your task in clear, specific terms.
Instead of getting overwhelmed with a big task like "write
a book," break it down into a feasible, specific set of steps
like "edit chapters seven and eight."

4.   Recall an instance of excellent performance.
Describe the details of a time when you executed a task
and had excellent results, like turning in a paper that got
an A+ or delivering a killer client presentation or finishing
a marathon in record time. Note how you felt after your
accomplishment.

5.   Set a specific goal for your performance.
Write in specific terms, like "I will deliver a powerful and
compelling talk to the twenty-five Realtors at the meeting"
or "I will write a clear e-mail of apology to my unhappy
customer, which will address his concerns and calm his
anger."

6.   Jump into the work for a short burst of time,
in a maximum of fifteen-minute segments. Give
it your all.

Do not judge your work while you are doing it. The important thing is to take your positive mind-set and clear goal and do the very best you can.

Fear is an essential part of the creative process. Work with it, and you will create a powerful, full-color, full-contact body of work.

CHAPTER 7

Collaborate

You will have everything in life you want, if you will just help other people get what they want.

—Zig Ziglar

Kyle Durand had accomplished a lot during his twenty years in the navy, his career as a postdoctorate tax attorney, and through his hobby of extreme sports. He had been deployed four times to the Middle East and had experienced two wars, had helped businesspeople untangle all kinds of legal messes, and had run a double marathon in South Africa for fun.

But he couldn't figure out how to bring his software idea to life.

As an attorney, he would draft legal agreements and e-mail them to his clients for review and signing. Often they would be agreements his clients would share with their clients, who would inevitably have edits and changes to the contract.

Very quickly, a simple agreement would turn into multiple e-mails back and forth, with redlines and text edits in the contract document. Once finalized, the document would have to be printed, signed, scanned, then sent back. The original client would print that document out, sign it, scan it, and finally return a copy to all parties.

Kyle wanted to build software that contained templates of legally sound contracts that creative professionals could use to do things like set up joint-venture agreements, audio-visual recording releases, bills of sale, and promissory notes. He envisioned a website where it would be possible to send, review, and digitally sign contracts with no fuss or headache.

The problem was that he had never created a software product and had no idea where to start.

When Kyle came to me with this problem, I suggested that he attend the Business of Software, a technology conference in Boston that brought together the best, most experienced and successful software startup founders in one place.

At the conference, Kyle learned the best practices for developing products, which tools to use to do the development, and mistakes to avoid.

After the conference, he read a pile of books and blog posts about software development.

With a better idea of what he wanted to build, Kyle now needed help building it.

He attended the first Lift Off Retreat that I ran with my partner, Charlie Gilkey. Lift Off was a three-day business-design retreat where we brought together thirteen entrepreneurs from all over the country to Saguaro Lake Ranch, in Mesa, Arizona.

When Kyle shared his idea with others in the group, he found that there was a small subset of retreat participants who had the exact skill sets he needed to build the first prototype of his product.

A couple of weeks later, Kyle decided to fly a small team of retreat participants—expert researcher Crystal Williams, graphic designer Rhiannon Llewellyn, videographer Karen Yaeger, and technology consultant Willie Jackson—to a rented house in the San Juan Islands near his home in Seattle. They bunkered down for five days and brainstormed and researched ideas on the spot. Rhiannon created wireframes as they sketched out the design, Crystal completed detailed research on various ideas, and Willie communicated with outside technology experts as they discussed different tools and programs.

By the end of the weekend, this small team had a basic business model, ideas about which technology to use, and wireframes to build on.

After the San Juan Islands retreat, Kyle and Willie interviewed a variety of software developers and other Lift Off participants, one of which knew a team of great developers in Buenos Aires.

Kyle and Willie decided to hire the Argentine team of developers, who quickly built the beta version of his software ourdeal.com, which now provides a quick and easy way for clients to review, edit, and digitally sign legal contracts.

Before this experience, Kyle was used to figuring things out on his own. He felt uncomfortable asking for help at first, but soon learned that identifying a strong peer network of friends and collaborators was a great way to reduce risk, develop ideas, and grow business. The original team is still friends and refers clients back and forth to one another.

Kyle did invest some money in bringing the team together to flesh out the original project, but it was much less than he would have paid to hire someone else to do the work, or worse, to just guess his way through building the software himself and make costly mistakes.

Because he went through the entire process, it was easy to later spin off new software projects, like taxreceipts.com, which helps entrepreneurs easily navigate tax code so that they know what kind of expenses are valid business write-offs, and part-nerright.com, which provides expert guidance on setting up joint ventures and partnerships.

Kyle learned that identifying and building strong collaborative partnerships with peers, experts, and mentors is a critical part of the formula for business success, especially when you are setting out to expand a specific aspect of your body of work.

Collaborating effectively is a key skill in the new world of work, no matter which work mode you choose.

Connectional intelligence—CxQ

Harvard researcher Erica Dhawan agrees that collaboration and peer networks are an essential part of the new world of work. She takes the discussion a step further and says that there is a new type of intelligence, as important as intellectual quotient (IQ) and emotional quotient (EQ), which she calls *connectional intelligence.*

"Connectional intelligence (CxQ) is the ability to build and realize value from networks of relationships, to harness units of knowledge and reuse them to innovate, to convene communities, [and] to marshal a variety of resources for break-through results. In the past decade, we've seen an exponential rise of CxQ as seen through millennials curating TEDx events via webcasts that reach millions; starting social businesses blending profit and purpose, like TOMS Shoes and Warby Parker; or using social sharing and crowd-funding tools, such as Kickstarter, to reach new audiences."

Erica and her collaborator, Saj-nicole Joni, chief executive of Cambridge International Group, consult with Fortune 500 companies to develop cross-generational dialogue and empower all employees to share their natural connectional intelligence to improve innovation in organizations. Their thirty-year age difference provides perspective and depth to the work they do as a team.

Saj-nicole says, "This generation is uniquely equipped to lead to breakthrough innovation in a way that has never before been possible, because it is the first to have grown up in a world of ubiquitous connection. For millennials, engagement with all social media is not only about entertainment or news. It is embedded in daily life. Digital connection is the air they breathe. They do everything in it, from deeply sharing their lives with friends and family (who may live in different cities or countries) to shopping and paying bills, communicating at work. . . .

"The missing link is this: In our new world of an embedded digital infrastructure that connects all of our lives, the *power of connectional intelligence holds exponential, and previously untapped, potential for breakthroughs* in ways we can barely begin to imagine."

Erica and Saj-nicole believe that contextual capacity—the ability to bring together different kinds of people and ideas to foster the recombination of different ideas, and to see things from a different perspective—is a key part of connectional intelligence and a key skill for both individuals and institutions to develop if they want to remain competitive.

In Erica's research at the Harvard Kennedy School of Government and in studies for their book, Erica and Saj-nicole are creating and encouraging "sparring zones"—places where people of very different backgrounds can discuss and debate ideas, in an open and healthy way.

By mobilizing networks to share ideas, they can create great things and solve big problems.

Erica says, "Globalization of business, economic, and political instability and global hyper-connectivity is forcing us to approach innovation and problem solving differently. Connectional intelligence is becoming a key differentiator in organizations who want to remain competitive."

I agree wholeheartedly with Erica and Saj-nicole.

For some people, this connectional intelligence comes naturally. For others, it is a skill to be learned.

The best way to learn about it is to understand avatars, ecosystems, and watering holes.

Avatars, ecosystems, and watering holes

Connecting is so much easier when you know the specific characteristics of ideal collaborators and where they spend their time. I define ideal collaborators as *avatars*, the broad networks where they hang out as *ecosystems*, and the specific locations where large numbers of avatars hang out as *watering holes*.

Depending on your work mode and business objective, you may be looking to connect with peers, mentors, clients, or customers.

Many people spread themselves too thin by spending hours trying to cultivate connections on social media or by attending multiple workshops and conferences, hoping that the right peers, mentors, and clients will magically appear. When you do the work to focus and clarify your ideal collaborators, you get much better results with less effort.

Ideal connection avatar

When you can describe the specific characteristics of people you want to collaborate with, it makes it much easier to find them. It will also make it easier to screen out people who are not the right fit.

Individual collaborators can be defined with some demographic information:

- Profession
- Income level
- Geographic area
- Psychographic characteristics (personality, values, vibe, et cetera)
- Age
- Gender
- Ethnicity
- Interests
- Hobbies

Institutional collaborators can be defined by things such as:

- Nature of business or organization
- Size of company

- Type of industry (high technology, manufacturing, health and wellness, et cetera)
- Geographic area

Alan Cooper originated the concept of Buyer Personas in his 1999 book, *The Inmates Are Running the Asylum*. In recent years, the more common term is "ideal client avatars." I am certain that Apple has my picture hanging on the white board of their marketing department. Under "Ideal Customer Avatar," they would have:

- Anglo female
- Forty-six years old
- Mother of small children
- Loves technology
- Loves design
- Loves TED, PopTech, Ignite
- Entrepreneur
- Heavy social media user

With this kind of specific description, there are all kinds of ways and places Apple could (and does) market to me. I am embarrassed to say it works: I have an iPhone, iPad, iMac, and MacBook Air.

Similarly to discovering your ideal client avatars, once you have clear descriptions of your ideal collaboration avatars, you are ready to define the ecosystem in which they live.

Ecosystems

No individual or company stands alone in its market. There are a whole group of other companies that market to the same people.

When I was teaching a marketing class about ecosystems and watering holes, I took to Twitter to ask who my followers thought would be in the Whole Foods Market ecosystem. I got back the following answers.

- Trader Joe's
- The Fresh Market
- REI
- Patagonia
- Rent A Goat
- TOMS Shoes
- Farmers' markets
- Yoga studios
- Pilates studios
- lululemon
- Honda
- Toyota (Prius)
- Volkswagen
- Apple
- TED.com
- Gaiam (organic clothes)
- Laura's Lean Beef

When I shared these findings on Twitter, I got this reply from my Canadian friend Lianne Raymond:

"I love Whole Foods mushroom blue cheese pizza (she

types into her Apple computer before driving her VW to yoga in her lululemon slit crop boogie pants).”

Without having any prior awareness, Lianne realized that she was smack in the middle of a brand ecosystem.

Watering holes

When you have a sense of your ideal connections and the overall ecosystem in which they participate, you can start to look for watering holes. These are places, online and in person, where large concentrations of your ideal connections hang out.

They include:

- Blogs
- Forums
- Conferences
- Events
- Stores

The South by Southwest Interactive Festival in Austin, Texas, is a watering hole for social media–active, technology-loving innovators. You can meet thousands of customers, peer collaborators, mentors, watering-hole gatekeepers, journalists, and corporate sponsors.

When I was standing in line for hours to register for the event in 2012, I struck up a conversation with a *Wall Street Journal* reporter from the San Francisco bureau. Later that evening, in one small hotel lobby bar, I met the vice president of a huge technology company, the owner of a 300,000-member marketing site, a viral video legend, and a famous bestselling author. Outside of a conference watering hole, it would have taken many headaches, unreturned e-mails, and conversations with gatekeepers to get this same level of access to this group of influential people.

Conferences are not the only effective watering holes. Blogs or online forums can also be excellent places to meet peers, mentors, and customers.

When I first started my coaching business, Guy Kawasaki's blog was the watering hole that led me to so many great friends and partners, including Stanford professor and author Bob Sutton, *Presentation Zen* author Garr Reynolds, author and programmer Kathy Sierra, and marketing expert Seth Godin. After Guy linked to a few of the posts on my blog, I got a flood of new subscribers, and it earned him the nickname of my "link sugar daddy." He ended up becoming a friend and wrote the foreword to my first book.

AVATARS, ECOSYSTEMS, AND WATERING HOLES

If you take the time to define your ideal connection avatars, ecosystems, and watering holes, your networks will grow exponentially faster. And as Kyle Durand discovered, you will be able to create and build new pieces of your body of work better and quicker.

To create your collaboration plan, follow these three steps:

1. Define the specific characteristics of your ideal connection avatar.

You may have more than one—try to capture the most important ones. Remember, ideal connections not only help you do your best work, but they are also *fun* to work with!

Demographic information: age, gender, cultural background, profession

Psychographic information: personality type, communication style, conative style

Special ingredients: skills, experience, values

2. Define the ecosystem that surrounds your ideal connection avatar.

Which products and services do they buy?

Whom are they influenced by? (authors, political leaders, cultural figures)

What do they read? (books, magazines, blogs)

3. Identify the watering holes where your ideal connections hang out.

Where will you find concentrated group of your ideal avatars within the ecosystems?

Be as specific as possible! "They hang out on blogs" will not help you get clients. Which blogs? Which live events?

Network roles: connector, maven, and salesman

Malcolm Gladwell has contributed many great ideas to the business world over the years with bestselling books like *Blink* and *Outliers*.

His book *The Tipping Point* changed the way I think about creating and developing networks that help develop and deploy great ideas into the world. In chapter 2, Gladwell describes three types of people:

- Connectors: People with the extraordinary gift of bringing large groups together
- Mavens: People with a vast amount of diverse knowledge
- Salespeople: People with the skills to persuade and spread information

When you identify your primary "Tipping Point Archetype," you know how to leverage your strength, and, most important, you identify the archetypes you need to surround yourself with in order to strengthen the quality of and to spread ideas for your body of work.

How do you recognize these types in the real world?

Connectors are fantastic at expanding your network. When you share your idea with them, they will say:

"Oh, you should talk to . . ."
"Have you heard about Bob, who wrote that book . . ."
"Let me introduce you to . . ."

They think in terms of people, and networks of people, and like nothing more than to help you.

Mavens will dig deeply into your product and give very specific, detailed, and relevant information on how it can fit within the marketplace.

"I was researching that last month, and I noticed a slight discrepancy in . . ."

"Your work fits right in the xxx part of yyy's essay on the zzz topic."

"You could add videos to this to bring the lessons alive! And you could expand on the content in chapter three, section two, by listing . . ."

Salesmen will take the idea and help you package it, price it, and sell it. They'll say:

"Here is one way that you could position it, in order to get people excited about the idea."

"What is the big idea? What is the promise?"

"You have to have an offer. Traffic means nothing if it doesn't lead to a sale."

"What is your pricing structure?"

"What specific value will this have to your market? How much is that worth?"

My friend Charlie Gilkey, who identifies as a maven, thinks that we have primary, secondary, and tertiary Tipping

Point Archetypes. So you could be a connector (primary), maven (secondary), and salesman (tertiary), relying on each of the strengths in differing quantities.

One fun way I like to help people figure out which is their primary network role is to ask a question like: "How would you get to the moon?" And take note of their instinctual response.

Connectors think of anyone they know who may know someone who works at NASA.

Mavens run through different scenarios and calculations to determine exactly what the task entails. Would they be flying in a rocket? Does NASA have any plans to fly to the moon, or are Mars and Jupiter more of a budget priority?

Salesmen think about what powerful story they could tell to convince Richard Branson that they are a great candidate for the next commercial airline flight to the moon.

How do you use network roles in the real world?

Executive coach Michele Woodward created the Connector Strategy Tool, which she uses to help clients conducting a job search identify the connectors in their life. One of Michele's clients who used the tool reported that after having lunch with a connector, he sent eight messages of introduction to hiring managers on her behalf by the time she got back to the office.

Charlie Gilkey and I used the network role model in our Lift Off Retreat, and it was exceptionally eye-opening for the participants, who realized: A) They should celebrate who they really are and ignore advice to change into something they are not. B) By surrounding themselves with other network roles, their businesses will grow to a whole other level.

CONNECTOR, MAVEN, OR SALESMAN

- Name your primary network role. Are you a connector, a maven, or a salesman? (If you are unsure where you fit, you can read more in Malcolm Gladwell's *The Tipping Point*.)
- Evaluate your current work model through this lens. Are you setting yourself up for success or failure? Connectors build bridges, mavens dig deep and research, and salesmen influence and sell. Is that what you are doing?
- Identify your missing network roles. Which parts of creating and sharing ideas are difficult for you? Who do you need more of in your life?
- In your next project, build a small well-rounded council with mavens, connectors, and salesmen. If you are inside a company, you might consider pulling in people from other divisions or departments to share perspectives. If you have your own company, you can organize a peer network to share ideas and information.

Who should you have in your networks?

I recommend that everyone have the following people in their network (in addition to your beloved spouse and kids/pets):

- Two people you can text at any time day or night
- Two mentors you can call when you have great challenges or opportunities
- A smart, challenging friend who will pick apart your ideas without crushing your confidence
- A best friend you can whine to, or celebrate with
- A strong, clear-thinking analytical friend who can help you solve complex problems
- A pocketful of creative thinkers who don't mind being pinged on the phone or Skype

Of course you can have a lot more people in your circle, but if you have these bases covered, you are in excellent shape.

What can real, live people do that books, videos, or your own brain cannot?

Hold you accountable

My friend Michael Bungay Stanier, author of *Do More Great Work*, took a keen interest in my own crazy writing process and volunteered to be my accountability partner for writing this book. Our methods included daily e-mail check-ins about the number of words written, as well as scattered Skype chats when I get stuck or overwhelmed. Knowing that Michael is investing his time in my success makes me feel extra motivated to get the book done.

Challenge your thinking

You want people in your life who will help you to think in new, different, and more nuanced ways. My friend Barbara Saunders always has a unique perspective on my work and takes the time to offer detailed comments. (Incidentally, our podcast interview about how we misjudge introverts is one of my most popular.)

Balance your strengths

Chances are, if you have tremendous strengths in one area (strategic thinking, graphic design, quantum physics), you also have noteworthy weaknesses in other areas. Highly detailed tax attorney Kyle Durand has done the unthinkable: made this liberal arts major get excited about legal contracts, partnership agreements, and watertight financial statements.

Remind you of your true path

Best friends, like my Desiree Adaway, remind you that no matter how dark the current moment appears, there is a better day ahead. People who know you very well have a unique perspective about your patterns and your true self.

Motivate you

Andy Pels refuses to let me do anything less than my best work. He immediately sends me an e-mail if I have a typo in a blog post. He actually prescheduled motivating e-mails last August to hit my in-box at the time when I was due to be finishing my book.

I have many more dear friends and trusted colleagues, but these are a few examples of the kind of people who can keep you moving forward, despite your valiant efforts to shrink back from your greatness.

Where can you find a support team?

If you don't already have strong circle of peers around you, I suggest looking for them:

- in organizations: work, college, spiritual, or hobby groups.
- in classes: often you can find great peers in online classes or programs.
- in your local community: look for Meetup groups, professional associations, coworking spaces, or conferences.
- online: fellow blog readers, Facebook buddies, Twitter pals, or LinkedIn connections are excellent sources of peer mentors.

A great circle of peer mentors reminds you that *we all need each other.*

When each of us operates from our strengths, invests in one another's successes, and sees the world as a series of creative collaborations, we all win.

You must still create your own success

While learning from the best and most successful in your field, it is very important to make sure you are not asking them to do your work for you. Martha Beck once told me: "Every time I go to a cocktail party, well-meaning authors or experts corner me with a copy of their book, asking in a hushed tone 'Would you mind giving my book to Oprah when you are in her office?' What they should be asking is: 'What were the most powerful steps you took to prepare yourself to be on *Oprah*?'"

Seth Godin said something very similar in his post "No Knight, No Shining Armor":

> The magic of the tribe is that you can build it incrementally, that day by day you can earn the asset that will allow you to bring your work to people who want it. Or you can skip that and wait to get picked. Picked to be on *Oprah* or *American Idol* or at the cash register at Borders.
>
> Getting picked is great. Building a tribe is reliable; it's hard work and it's worth doing.

The eight magic questions, not the magic bullet

So what is your brand-new business idea or big goal that you have no idea how to accomplish?

Getting a book deal? Breaking into a new market? Getting a job in a different industry? Creating a successful software product? Getting your own television show? Monetizing your blog?

Answer the following questions:

- Who has done this, or something similar to this, and done it well?
- Of all the people I find who have done this well, which of them share my values, work ethic, and life goals?
- What were the key moves these people made in order to have success?
- Who are the deep experts, enthusiasts, and influential people in this area?
- Where do they hang out, so I can go meet them?

- What criteria do decision makers use to select products or projects? (Most relevant for things like book deals, television shows, getting venture capital, or being chosen for guest posts on popular blogs.)
- How can I apply this learning to my own business planning?
- What are my key moves in the next month, next quarter, and next year to get me to my goal as quickly as possible?

The more you develop your network, the more ease you will feel when starting new or challenging projects.

How to ask for help when you get stuck

I work with a lot of smart people. Folks who have done amazing things in their careers, raised great children, changed their communities, created fine pieces of art, and solved complex problems.

As they are attempting something new, they often hit a wall if they can't figure it out. Many get paralyzed and lose confidence and momentum the longer they don't have an answer.

Some of this is based on assumptions they make about what people think of those who ask for help.

Common assumptions about asking for help in a competitive environment:

- If you ask for help, you are weak.
- Smart people are too busy to help.
- Asking for help is a nuisance.

- If you ask for help, no one will trust you.
- If you ask for help, you are not an expert.

Common assumptions about asking for help in the new world of entrepreneurship:

- If you ask for help, you want to learn.
- People love to share their expertise; it helps them to feel valued and validated.
- Asking for help is the quickest way to grow a business, solve a problem, and attain your goals.

When you are in a stuck place and feel overwhelmed, the one thing that will not make you feel better is spending more time alone thinking. You will go from:

"I cannot figure out how to write this proposal!" to "I will never be able to write this proposal!" to "Who was I to ever think that I had any right to be in business?"

It is a very ugly spiral.

To avoid this, you need to get used to asking for help early and often.

The key to getting great help is to make the request *clear* and *brief.* Write your questions in a form that will allow someone to give a brief and specific answer.

Good Technique: "Hey, Pam, do you know anyone who specializes in local business marketing strategies?"

As opposed to:

Bad Technique: "Hey, Pam, how should I market my business?"

This kind of broad question makes my head spin and is really hard to answer with a brief e-mail.

Five ways to ask for help
1. Describe what you need help with in clear language.

> "I have a great software product, but I have no idea which conference to speak at in the New York area to attract ideal customers."

> "I need to change the header on my WordPress site, but I don't know how to do it."

> "I need to get my own health insurance, but I don't know where to get started."

2. Send a Tweet.
I consider Twitter an interesting alternative to Google because I get answers from people who share a personal connection. If you do not have a big Twitter following yet, ask someone who does. I constantly poll my Twitter circle with questions from friends and clients. Make sure your question is clear, brief, and includes "thanks."

Example: "Does anyone know a great health insurance broker in the Seattle area? Thanks in advance!"

3. Use LinkedIn Answers.
LinkedIn is full of smart and helpful people who can answer a whole range of professional questions. If someone answers your question, be sure to thank them, extend an invitation to

connect, and let them know you are available to answer questions for them as well.

4. Attend free calls and webinars.
I have been hosting a free monthly call for the past three years on my blog. I get a huge range of questions, and there are no strings attached to participating. Look for similar offers in your market—companies often host free training on their products, and other coaches or consultants do the same. Sometimes you will be pitched to buy something at the end, but that is a reasonable price to pay for free information.

5. Ask friends and colleagues from your professional organizations or programs.
You may have a great connection with someone who attends a monthly networking meeting you go to, or is in an educational program that you participate in. Send a direct message to them, and see if they can help you. Some of these early exchanges can lead to more extended learning partnerships, like masterminds. I met Philippa Kennealy, from the Entrepreneurial MD, in a program run by Andrea Lee, and after some brief exchanges, she and I became mastermind partners for the whole first year we started our blogs (way back in 2005!). She is a big reason why I got early momentum and success on my blog.

Asking for help, and giving help on a consistent basis, is the best thing you can do for your body of work. It doesn't have to be a lonely grind; it can be a rich exchange of ideas, information, and resources.

How to manage a growing network

When you begin to cultivate your network and build your connections, while it provides great diversity and "contextual capacity," it can quickly get overwhelming. People ask me quite often how I can keep up relationships with so many people as my in-person and virtual network grows.

The short answer is: I can't.

It would be pretty impossible to keep track of thirty-five thousand people on Twitter and hundreds of students and clients.

I do, however, get great joy from knowing a lot of people. Here are my tips for managing a growing network without burning out.

10 ways to strengthen connections with your network

1. Know your wing span.

As we discussed earlier, you can separate people into connectors, mavens, and salesmen. Connectors, if you remember, *love* to connect people and often have very large networks. I am a big connector, so every time I meet someone new, I think, "Cool! Someone else who can be a resource to my community!" If you are not a connector, you may need to define the maximum size network that feels comfortable for you. Kevin Kelly's concept of one thousand true fans may appeal to more introverted people who would rather have depth than breadth in their network.

2. Change your expectations.

If you expect that you will remember to write personal birthday cards to every single person in your network, you will be massively stressed out. The nature of social networks is that they are loose, open, and instantaneous. Instead of thinking, "I must keep tabs on every single thing each person is doing," you can think, "I will make sure to really pay attention to the people who come across me today." You do not have to have deep, long conversations with everyone every week in order to consider them a friend and advocate.

3. Choose your inner circle.

I have a very small circle of people who I call on all the time. I make it a priority to stay very connected with their lives and rely on them to help me with my own challenges. Being thoughtful about who is in this very small circle means I have more energy to reach out and connect with a lot more people from a more grounded perspective.

4. Love the one you're with.

When you have the opportunity to meet someone at a live event, give them your full attention. Plant your feet. Look them in the eyes. Listen to what they are saying. Recently, at the World Domination Summit in Portland, Oregon, I was in a room with more than three thousand people. I wanted to talk to all of them. But since that was not possible, I made sure to really connect with each person I did talk to, even if it was only for two minutes in the hallway.

5. Sprinkle in random check-ins.

I love to jump on a quick video chat and surprise a friend, pop by a new blog, or start up a conversation on Twitter with someone I don't know well. These are often brief conversations, but they form a strong connection for a few minutes and often bridge into feeling comfortable with that person when you meet him or her in real life. I also love scanning through my phone contact list and doing random "Hello, I miss you" calls when I have a few extra minutes.

6. Set expectations for communication.

I send a note to everyone who joins my newsletter asking for their biggest question about starting a business. I use this technique to gather data about blog posts to write or classes to create. I write, "I may not be able to answer each question individually, but I do host a free call the first Wednesday of the month, which you are welcome to join." Many sign up for the calls and not only get their questions answered but also hear useful information from others. On my blog, I do not set the expectation that I will respond to every comment, because that would not work with the limited amount of time I dedicate to work each day. I do set the expectation that I will read and enjoy every comment or question. Expectations give everyone room to breathe.

7. Prioritize critical people in your network like bosses, clients, close friends, or family members.

A couple of years ago I got an e-mail from a client who felt like I was not checking in enough with what she was up to. Do you know what? She was right. Listening to what she needed from me reminded me that it is a privilege to be a coach, and I should make adjustments in my work flow to make sure I follow the work of my clients more closely than that of my broader network. I am very appreciative of her feedback as it affected the way I structure my client relationships.

8. Use technology.

You can create groups on Twitter (of clients, of friends, of favorite thinkers) so you can have a small and focused window into key segments of your network. If you scan the stream of these special groups, you can respond, retweet, and encourage in an organized manner. You can also set reminders in your calendar at different times of the month to e-mail current clients, or to stop by the blogs of your favorite folks. Knowing that you have a block of time to check up on key networks will stop you from feeling pressured to do so every day.

9. Connect people with each other.

I believe that my main purpose is to create community. I don't want to create a situation where everyone is lined up trying to talk with me; I want them to talk with each other. So think about the best dinner party host you know—what do they do? They invite great people to the party. They serve great food. They make the environment open and inviting. They introduce people to each other. Then they slip into the kitchen to make more hors d'oeuvres so that everyone can start talking.

10. Get meta.

I love meditations where I visualize sending love to all of the people and creatures on earth. Feeling the pulse of collective humanity reminds me that we are always connected by virtue of sharing the same planet. We do not have to talk with each person on earth to know that—we can feel it.

As Kyle found out, creating a network of the right people with the right skill sets can be the difference between simmering an idea for years without doing anything about it and executing real, live projects that improve the quality of life for people you care about.

This chapter should help you feel less overwhelmed and more joyful about your connections and collaborations. Remember to trust your instincts. Creating your body of work can be a daunting task. Don't think you have to build it alone.

Exercise: Identify a Peer Mentor Circle

For your next project, experiment with creating a peer mentor circle, composed of people who can give you support, feedback, and ideas.

Name of project: _____

Objective: _____

Your strengths and special ingredients as they relate to this project: _____

_____

Your weaknesses, unknowns, and skill gaps as they relate to this project: _____

_____

Names of five people you know who could help address these weaknesses, unknowns, and skill gaps: _____

_____

_____

Means of communication you will use to solicit input from your peer mentors for this project: (e-mail, video conferencing, in-person meeting, et cetera)_____

_____

Length of project: _____

_____

How you will thank your mentors for giving you feedback: ___

_____

_____

CHAPTER 8

Your Definition of Success

> Don't aim at success—the more you aim at it and make
> it a target, the more you are going to miss it. For success,
> like happiness, cannot be pursued; it must ensue, and it
> only does so as the unintended side-effect of one's
> dedication to a cause greater than oneself.
> —Viktor E. Frankl, *Man's Search for Meaning*

John Stephens grew up in a working-class family in Spring-field, Ohio. His father was a factory worker, and his mother a part-time seamstress. Passionate about education and frustrated with the public school options in her neighborhood, his mother homeschooled him on and off until the age of twelve, when he started high school as a child prodigy.

His grandmother had taught him to play piano, and he began to sing in church at age seven and write songs at age eleven.

He graduated from high school as salutatorian at age sixteen. He was recruited by schools like Harvard and Georgetown but chose to attend the University of Pennsylvania, where he graduated magna cum laude. His passion for education, nurtured by his mother, showed in his own dedication to his academic career, as well as in his interest in social justice and education advocacy.

John continued to pursue his passion for music in the evenings and weekends, playing in clubs in Philadelphia, Atlanta, New York, and Washington, DC.

After graduating from college, he took a job as a management consultant at Boston Consulting Group. He was known for his shy manner and excellent capability in Microsoft Excel.

A former coworker, Jane Park, raved about his skills: "I used to work with John Stephens when he was a consultant at BCG. He was lovely and brilliant and built Excel spreadsheets like there was no tomorrow. But he also seemed quiet and I would have characterized him as an introvert. He taught me how to build complex models using buttons in Excel (for predicting the likelihood of success of early-stage pharmaceuticals). He always had his headset on—he sang softly while he worked."

After being a supporting player for many musicians as the side hustle to his day job, John finally got a big break after meeting Kanye West. West produced John's first solo album, *Get Lifted*, which went on to win three Grammy Awards, including Best New Artist.

John Stephens, the quiet, smart management consultant who loved to sing, changed his name to John Legend at the suggestion of his friend, poet J. Ivy, and with nine Grammys to his name, became an international superstar.

Jane Park admits she had no idea of the star potential of her former coworker. Convinced that he was destined for a quiet career as an analyst, she doubted his ability to interact with customers. Describing her thoughts at the time, she said, "He'll never make it in client services. I thought, 'He doesn't have much of a personality.' Now, when I watch him emerge out of a cloud of dry ice, bursting with . . . personality, I eat my words."

After achieving fame and fortune, John Legend's commitment to education reform and social justice increased. With his public profile and abundant resources, he:

- founded the nonprofit Show Me Campaign to fight poverty and address the issue of education reform in the United States.
- hosted the PBS special TED series on education.
- appears in the press to talk about the importance of education reform, often in partnership with peers like the Harlem Village Academies, where he is a board member.
- uses his social media platform to interact with his fans and to support his political and social causes.

So why did the gifted John Stephens give up a safe and secure business career to pursue an uncertain music career as John Legend?

When he got famous and rich, why didn't John Legend leave behind the passion John Stephens had for education and social justice?

I think it is because he has a definition of success that incorporates his roots, leverages all of his ingredients, and builds a body of work that his fans and parents can be proud of.

You do not have to become an international superstar to have a rich and meaningful life. You do not have to give up a rich and meaningful life to become an international superstar.

Get clear on your definition of success and how you can use it to grow your body of work.

Success in the new world of work

How do you define true success?

This question has plagued academics, artists, parents, teachers, and businesspeople for centuries. It has spawned hundreds of motivational posters and thousands of quotes. I have rarely met a person in my life who does not want to feel successful.

Personally, I define success as enjoying my life while I am living it. Which means living in accordance with my values, doing work that matters, being available to my loved ones, and staying focused and mindful in the present, instead of wishing for success in the future.

But success is different for everyone. What does success mean to you? How do we know if we have reached the pinnacle of success? And how do you shape a body of work that leads to a successful outcome?

I was scanning my news feed one morning and a headline jumped out from businessinsider.com: "The 'Real Winners of the World' Don't Have Work-Life Balance, They Have Work."

In the article, career coach Marty Nemko said: "The real winners of the world, the people that are the most productive, think that this notion of work-life balance is grossly overrated. Most of the highly successful and not-burned-out people I know work single-mindendly towards a goal they think is important, whether it's developing a new piece of software, inventing something, or a cardiologist who's seeing patients on nights and weekends instead of playing Monopoly with his kids on the weekend."

I felt the heat rise in my face as I saw the term "real winner" equated with someone who avoids playing with his kids so he can concentrate on work.

I judged him. Hard. "Why in the world would you even have kids, if you are just going to ignore them?"

And then I realized, in a more calm moment, that my view of parenting may not be any more "right" than said cardiologist because everyone has a very different take on what it means to be a good (successful) parent.

I was actually more bothered by the idea that there are "real winners" of the world and that one definition of success can be viewed as better than another, while ignoring the real tradeoffs of choosing one path over another.

How do you lean into success?

In her bestselling book *Lean In*, Facebook COO Sheryl Sandberg argues that women have been sabotaging their own success for years by building internal barriers that limit upward mobility in their careers. Many people misinterpreted her premise as saying that all women *must* push higher up the career ladder.

In fact, she says, "I do not believe that there is one definition of success and happiness. Not all women want careers. Not all women want children. Not all women want both. I would never advocate that we should all have the same objectives. Many people are not interested in acquiring power, not because they lack ambition, but because they are living their lives as they desire."

In the years I have worked on helping people leave their cubicles to start their own businesses, I saw reverse snobbism against people who chose to remain employees in large companies.

"You are not really free unless you work for yourself," entrepreneurs would say.

Really? Say that to a terrified and exhausted entrepreneur, unsure if he can pay his mortgage next month but too embarrassed to get a job, lest his friends think he is a loser for giving up too soon.

"You are only a cog in a machine if you work for someone else."

But what if you have the opportunity to work for dynamic people, creating great things, in an organization that provides a competitive salary, full health benefits, retirement savings, and three weeks paid vacation that you can use to travel the world or spend time with those you love?

Common career advice

There is a lot of career advice that people feel very strongly about.

- If you have a traditional career, you must climb the ladder.
- If you are a strong individual contributor, you must become a manager.
- If you are a successful entrepreneur, you must scale your business.

- If you make a lot of money, you should make even more money.
- If you achieve fame and success, you should push for a bigger stage.

There are common beliefs that keep people feeling trapped, defensive, or guilty about their choices

- If you are a woman or minority and are successful, it is because you were given breaks, not because of the quality of the work that you do.
- If you are from the majority and are successful, it is because you were given unfair advantages.
- If you have a well-paying job, you should be grateful for it and not risk stability to run a business. If you start your own business and find it doesn't suit you, you should keep pressing forward because once you leave your job, it is too embarrassing to come back.
- If you have kids, you should not work all the time, so you can be a better parent.
- If you are a parent, you should demonstrate high standards and excellence to your kids by achieving career success.

What definition of success do you believe?
I recently sat on a plane next to a gentleman who had come to the United States from India in 1984. He told me, with a very heavy heart, how his son was in college and "spent his weekends with his peers working on ideas for online businesses."

"He is throwing away his education," he said. "Why doesn't he focus all his attention and energy on his career and become the best engineer he can be? That is what is wrong with this country now; we are losing our competitive edge."

I listened to him very patiently for more than an hour. I was too chicken to tell him that I was the author of *Escape from Cubicle Nation* and was working on a new book about how putting all your aspirations in a single career path was a risky career choice in the new world of work. I imagined how challenging the dynamic was between father and son when it came to career discussions.

And yet, listening to the passion in the father's voice when he talked about his views on work made me think that he and his son had more in common than they might believe. "I love math," he said. "And I am helping some of the employees at my neighborhood Starbucks with their math homework."

While he did not agree with his son's approach to education, he did take pride in his craft and was truly concerned about excellence. I like to think that if I had been on a longer flight, I might have been able to change his mind.

When I told this story to some of my Indian friends, they laughed at my naïveté. Some family and cultural definitions of success are not open to discussion and debate, nor likely to change. For many people, pleasing their parents is a strong and significant part of their specific success criteria.

If there is no agreement on societal standards of success, if you choose not to be swayed by biases, and if your parents have opinions about career that you do not agree with, how do you know what true success is?

You must create your own definition.

Body of Work Success Framework

Your Body of Work Success Framework draws from everything we have talked about so far.

Your roots

What is deeply important to you, inherently interesting, and intrinsically motivating?

Who do you want to impact and why?

(Remember Amanda Wang's determination to succeed in chapter 2, fueled by her commitment to ease suffering of BPD patients and their families.)

Your ingredients

Which projects utilize a compelling mix of your ingredients, leverage your strengths, and continually allow you to learn, grow, and develop?

(Remember David Batstone's unique combination of ingredients in chapter 3, which helped him successfully found an antislavery organization.)

Your handling of fear and doubt

What have you learned about yourself that will help if you get scared or feel pressure? How can you work with fear effectively so that you are still able to create and contribute to your body of work? (Remember Rafe Eric Biggs from chapter 7 and his ability to remain positive and productive through a devastating injury.)

Your work mode

Are you working as an employee, self-funded activist, academic, freelancer, or entrepreneur or multipotentialite?

Which standards of success do you want to measure? (Job performance rating, impact on your audience, number of projects completed, annual sales, or enthusiasm for rate of personal and professional growth)

(Remember Emilie Wapnick from chapter 4 and her passion for having multiple work modes and projects.)

Your creation

What are you creating now (e.g., a product, a degree, a book, an album, a movement)? What does completion look like? What standard are you using to measure the quality of the creation? (Number of units sold, grade point average, awards, number of comments or followers)

(Remember Mike Carson's passion for video and stage production in chapter 5, and the importance of creating work that will get you noticed, on his path to success.)

Your quality of life

How much money do you need to cover your financial needs? Are you a minimalist who is happy with few material objects? Or are you a maximist who is only happy with lots of material objects?

How much additional money do you want to invest in your own pleasure pursuits, the growth of your business, or the service of others?

How much money do you want to have in reserve for uncertain financial times, job loss, business, or retirement?

Your relationships and collaborations

What kind of friend, spouse, parent, and community member do you want to be?

Who do you need to have around you to ensure that you do your best thinking and complete projects that are important to you?

How much time do you want to invest in your relationships?

How many relationships can you sustain and still have time to rest, recover and create?

(Remember Kyle Durand from chapter 7 and his team of collaborators who helped him finally complete his software project.)

Your emotional and physical well-being

How do you want to feel when you wake up in the morning?

Where do you derive true emotional well-being and satisfaction?

Which conditions will drive optimal physical and emotional health?

After you've completed this exercise, you may find that your expectations in each of the categories are in direct conflict with each other.

That's perfectly normal.

If certain areas compete, which is a priority right now? Which sacrifices are you willing to make to serve your priorities?

QUICK DEFINITION OF SUCCESS

Sometimes, you just need a quick checklist when trying to decide which projects will give you the most satisfaction.

Does this project allow me to:

❑ meet my financial goals?

❑ use my strengths to create products I am proud of?

❑ enjoy the work while I am doing it?

❑ construct the life I want to live?

❑ serve people I care about and add value to the market?

Success dysmorphia

You may think that if you take the time to complete your Body of Work Success Framework, you will be perfectly content and satisfied when you reach your goals.

But if you are anything like me, you may temporarily forget your own success metrics and covet someone else's results.

When bestselling author Brené Brown was featured in two successive episodes of Oprah's *Super Soul Sunday*, you could feel the collective pangs of jealousy from authors everywhere, knowing the power Oprah has to move books.

After discussing *Daring Greatly*, Oprah looked at her and said with love, "You are my *soul mate*!"

While I would love for Oprah to call me her soul mate, what is important to remember is that Brené:

- spent years of her life doing unglamorous academic research.
- bared her soul and deepest insecurities to an audience of millions with her TED talk.
- wrote a fantastic, funny, carefully researched, and extremely accessible book on a topic relevant to a huge target audience.
- invested in her platform and speaking career in a way that she was prepared to deliver a truly riveting two-hour conversation with one of the best interviewers in the world.

Success dysmorphia is viewing your success through someone else's results and finding yourself feeling awkward, ugly, less than, and not quite on par with their accomplishments.

When you view your success through someone else's mirror

- There is always something bigger. Oprah was not content with a massively successful television show, she needed a network.
- You can always make more money. Carlos Slim, the world's richest man and hopefully a distant relative, always wants to increase his wealth.
- There is always someone with a hotter body. Demi

Moore spent years obsessing over her rock-hard, shapely figure.

- There is always someone who sells more books. Not content with creating a movement with *The 4-Hour Workweek*, Tim Ferriss smashed sales with his follow-up books *The 4-Hour Body* and *The 4-Hour Chef.*

- There is always someone who is a more productive parent. My client, lawyer Rachel Rodgers, was on bed rest for the last third of her pregnancy but still managed to care for her daughter, garner national press, serve her clients, and write a book just days before giving birth.

It's time for a new mirror

Measure your success using your own success framework.

Celebrate your accomplishments, even if they are different than your peers.

And own your choices. Respect your peers, and yourself, by saying, "I know I missed my daughter's dance recital, but I aced my client meeting and got the new account, which means that we will be able to go to Hawaii for vacation this year, just like I discussed with her."

Or "I sold 25,000 books to my friend's 250,000, but I was able to spend only half my time working and the other half of my time traveling the world."

Or "I am still twenty pounds heavier than my best friend, who looks amazing since she started training CrossFit five nights a week. But I have found a way to walk twenty minutes a day, even while working a full-time job and going to school at night. When I finish school and have more time to work out, I look forward to getting my washboard abs back."

Take pride in your accomplishments and notice how they become a source of pride in your body of work.

Your definition of success

I had a very interesting coaching conversation with a bright young woman. We were talking about her desire to expand her business and play bigger in the world.

When I asked what would happen if she started to put herself out in the world in a bigger way by offering more programs and connecting with more people, she got kind of quiet. I asked her what it would mean to her life if she grew her business. This is what she said:

"I would have to be out there with people all the time and wouldn't be able to spend days at home reenergizing." (She is an introvert according to the Myers Briggs test, which means she needs time alone to recharge her battery)

"I would ramp up my business, then if I decided to have kids, it would be hard to give that up so I could focus on being a mom.

"I would have to have all the answers and I am not sure I do."

I listened to her, and realized that she had very strong ideas about what it meant to be a *leader*. And I wasn't sure that this definition of leadership was one she wanted for herself; it was the model that she saw practiced by people she viewed as "successful."

So our homework assignment was to come up with a definition of leadership that *only applied to her life and situation*. It was OK if she wanted to be known as a leader who worked one day a month. It was also OK if she wanted to lead by having the freedom to change her mind frequently.

Your definition of success will drive who you serve and what you create, but, most important, how you feel while you are creating it.

I define success as enjoying my life while I am leading it. And I demonstrate leadership of my own life by:

- working only on projects that energize me and are connected with the body of work I want to create.
- contributing something useful to the global discussion of what work means in the twenty-first century.
- serving my roots by highlighting and supporting talented people from diverse backgrounds who are often overlooked by mainstream business and media.
- not working more than my body can handle.
- actively looking for fun and joy in work.
- taking joy and pride in being a parent and wife and being available to my kids and husband when they need me.
- being open to feedback and coaching in areas of weakness and fear.
- representing myself in a way that makes my mother, grandmother, and daughter proud.
- holding love and compassion in the highest priority.

Do I do *all* of these *every* day? Rarely. But this vision of leadership feels right to me. I am sure your list will be very different, but I hope it feels right to you.

So what does success mean to you?

I asked a group of my blog readers and clients to share their definitions of success. Here are some of their replies:

Glenda Watson Hyatt, a Canadian writer, consultant, and motivational speaker, was born with cerebral palsy due to lack of oxygen at birth. She has limited physical mobility and some significant speech impediments, but with a will of steel and supportive parents, she has learned to work within her physical parameters. Beyond writing her book with only her left thumb and giving speeches through speech translation software, Glenda views success this way:

"To me, success means working with my limitations or finding ways around them to lead a happy and fulfilled life. This means finding a balance between appreciating and being grateful for what I do have in that moment while still trying to improve my situation. Oftentimes it means getting creative to get something done or to increase my potential. For example, even though I have created a way to deliver a presentation to an audience, which in itself is amazing, and I am truly grateful to have that ability added to my repertoire, I will continue striving for a more graceful technical solution to deliver my message. For me that would be success."

Freelance writer and sometime stand-up comic Benjamin Gran defines success as:

"Freedom. Lots and lots of time with my wife and kids.

Not having to take crap from anyone. Not having to do stupid corporate busywork. Getting paid to express myself creatively."

Casey Barber, a food writer, says:

"Other than being able to pay the mortgage without waking up in night sweats? I'd say it's being able to proudly tell someone what you do at a cocktail party rather than feeling like you're boring them or waving it off as something you're almost ashamed of. Awards are great, but it's the sustained feeling of accomplishment that makes it possible to get through the day-to-day."

Chris Horner, a branch manager for a Community Bank, defines success as:

"Having time, resources, and energy to do what I want to do once obligations are done. Raising a responsible, appreciative family. A Ferrari would be nice too but is not mandatory."

Software developer Mike Tefft says:

"I would measure success as doing something you're passionate about while making sure that you can live the life you want. By that, I mean that you have time for family, friends, . . . life. You're not spending continual long hours of work at the expense of family and friends. You have enough money to support yourself with a little left over for some fun. And I think a little external recognition would probably help validate it. Many of us can't believe that we're actually good at something and a little external recognition from someone outside of your circle of family and friends tells you you're doing something right."

Nader Mahtabfar is a licensed dispensing optician who defines success as:

"Being able to overcome issues and challenges in an effort to do something remarkable so that many people can benefit."

Shari Risoff is a consultant to small businesses. Her definition of success:

"Pleasing God in my choices. Using the talents I have to provide solutions and help people."

Scott Barr is a finance manager for a local real estate company. He defines success as:

"On a more spiritual level, it would be happiness; on a more competitive level, it would be doing better than others in whatever category I'm being measured in (either by peers, mentally, by family). So if I have a better car, a better position at the local company, kids who are doing better, et cetera, then I'm succeeding—at least more than everyone else!"

Natalie Currie is a consultant and coach from Canada, with a passion for sustainability. Her definition of success reflects her maven nature:

"Paulo Coelho said it best: 'It is being able to go to bed each night with your soul at peace.'"

While there are some common themes in these definitions of success, it's obvious that a unique set of values has led to the creation of each one. Competition and challenge is motivating to one person, while personal freedom is important to another. Some need to feel passion for the work itself, while others value the time, resources, and opportunities they get from completing a job.

There is *no right answer.* There is only the answer that deeply resonates with you.

A personal reflection on success

> Over the years, I have come to realize that the greatest
> trap in our life is not success, popularity, or power, but
> self-rejection. Success, popularity, and power can in-
> deed present a great temptation, but their seductive
> quality often comes from the way they are part of the
> much larger temptation to self-rejection. When we
> have come to believe in the voices that call us worth-
> less and unlovable, then success, popularity, and power
> are easily perceived as attractive solutions. . . . Self-
> rejection is the greatest enemy of the spiritual life be-
> cause it contradicts the sacred voice that calls us the
> "Beloved." Being the Beloved constitutes the core
> truth of our existence.
>
> —Henri J.M. Nouwen

In 2010, I was invited to do a guest post for my friend Hugh
MacLeod, who is an artist and author. He was running a blog
series called "Remember Who You Are." As I thought about the
topic, it occurred to me that remembering the grace of who you
are in your most innocent state, outside of any personal or professional situation, is the most pure form of success.

So I wrote a very personal piece about my parents' divorce,
before my dad moved to Port Costa. Although the piece is
about my own journey back to myself, I also see it as the journey of both of my parents, who moved through the pain of
divorce to build strong and wonderful new marriages. Success
and happiness does not mean that we do not have periods of

intense pain and angst. Perhaps those times remind us who we really are. And what could be more successful than that?

YOU, LESS THAN

I still remember the smell of damp ivy from a recent rain as I stood in the backyard, waiting for my dad to take my picture.

It was 1971 and I was five years old. I was wearing a brightly colored knit vest, a present from my grandma. I tied my shoes myself but was not totally sure I had them on the right feet. It didn't matter. I was one powerful little girl. The Champion of the World.

My dad smiled at me, squinting his eyes as he crouched behind the camera. I was safe, cherished, and loved. He snapped the picture.

Things blew up after that, rather quickly.

My dad left home, and his marriage, to find himself. That's what people did in the 1970s in Marin County, California.

My world of family dinners and Dr. Seuss bedtime stories in my dad's lap ended. It was scary, unfamiliar, off-balance.

The way I had known myself—child of happy parents, member of a "normal" family—was no longer.

I spent a lot of time trying to figure out who I was. I tried to be a perfect student. And

when that got to be too much, I inhaled, a lot.
In my twenties I fell into a treacherous lover's
arms and paid dearly with a broken heart and
wounded soul.

I found martial arts, self-employment, and
writing.

And one day in a box full of old family
photographs, I found the picture.

Holding the yellowed edges in my hands, I
remembered who I was. I felt who I was. Who
I had always been, except when I forgot.

Circumstances can cause you to question
who you are.

A boss writes you a stinging performance
review.

A reader leaves a bitter comment on your
blog post.

A vocal audience member questions your
authority in the middle of your presentation.

A publisher sends back your treasured
manuscript with a crass note.

A spouse berates your manhood, or
womanhood.

And you go from You, the Champion of the
World to . . .

You, less than.

You, squashed.

You, angry and off-balance.

You, the misfit.

You, the screwup.

When you fall into this deep pit of treachery and despair, you need something to pull you out. An image, a word, a note. It helps when this object reflects both the love you have for yourself as well as the love someone has for you.

Like a picture of you through your parents' eyes.

Or a note from an impassioned reader who loved the piece that you loved to write. Or a rock from a beach that was so beautiful you could swear that the sand was kissing your feet.

You, less than, is a lie.

Remember who you are.

CHAPTER 9

Share Your Story

> Each of us chooses the tone for telling his or her own story. I would like to choose the durable clarity of a platinum print, but nothing in my destiny possesses the luminosity. I live among diffuse shadings, veiled mysteries, uncertainties; the tone of telling my life is closer to that of a portrait in sepia.
>
> —Isabel Allende, *Portrait in Sepia*

I remember hearing her voice choke up on the phone call.

"Once again, they told me I was overqualified for the job."

Desiree Adaway, my best friend since college, was at the end of her rope. She was part of a group layoff of consultants at Arthur Andersen, and for the past eight months had been sending her résumé everywhere. But no one was biting.

She had an amazing background and was one of the smartest people I knew. She was an exceptional manager, inspiring and mentoring those who worked for her. When she used to run children's camps, I would marvel at her ability to build a great relationship with every kind of kid as well as command the respect and trust of the teenage camp counselors.

As a project manager for IBM, she was trusted and respected by her peers and valued by her manager for her ability to get things done efficiently and on time. She would jump into new industries and drink up knowledge, fed by her interest in research and thirst for learning.

But there was something about the way she was presenting her experience that was not connecting with companies that were hiring.

I did a quick search online for resources to help Desiree, and Louise Garver, a career coach and résumé expert in Connecticut, stood out immediately. She offered a job-search package that included drafting a résumé and cover letter as well as doing targeted research to determine the organizations that would be a good fit. Desiree contacted her right away.

"When I first looked at Desiree's résumé, I didn't see any focus," Louise said. "Early in her career, she had experience with nonprofits and then in corporate environments, but I didn't see the connections between the two. I also didn't have any idea of her specific skills and strengths and how she had used them to make real and measurable impact in past jobs."

The first thing Louise did was to clarify Desiree's career target. What specific position did she want, in which industry? Then they gathered information, sample job postings, and used tools to identify key words and common denominators in the job responsibilities of her desired positions.

Next Desiree pulled out specific examples in her career history where she had addressed significant problems and had quantifiable outcomes. They dug into her natural patterns in any job, regardless of the situation. They found she was an exceptional problem solver and gifted manager. They examined what people always went to her for, if they were in a meeting or a project. Then they built strong stories around those examples.

With a crystal-clear job strategy, brand-new cover letter, and targeted résumé, Desiree hit the job market again.

Within a month, she had three ideal job offers. She took the position of global grants manager for the Rotary Foundation, where she oversaw millions of dollars of humanitarian grants all over the world. After a few years at Rotary, she moved to Habitat for Humanity, where she was senior director of volunteer mobilization.

Was it magic?

It sure felt like it to us.

In retrospect, it was really just a new spin on a truthful, powerful story, told in such a way that it both empowered the storyteller and excited the audience.

Desiree just hadn't taken the time to really consider the power of her entire body of work.

Now that we've done the heavy lifting of digging into your roots, ingredients, and work mode; discussed difficult topics like creativity and fear; and defined how you will measure your success, it's time to enter the last step: How do you tie it all together to create a compelling story and a marketable package?

No matter how wonderful and fulfilling your body of work is, if you want people to believe in it, act on it, be moved by it, or buy it, you must shape it into a cohesive narrative and tell powerful stories.

EXAMPLE OF A SUCCESS STORY

Just like she did with Desiree, Louise Garver gives an example of how she built a success story with a client with upgrade store management systems experience using these five questions.

1. What was the situation/problem you walked into that needed to be addressed?

The company spent $500 million per year on hourly labor and used a system that was designed to schedule labor for commission sales force. The hourly labor is not "self-funded" like commission, so labor has to be closely matched to customer demand and other work that takes place in the store.

2. What did you do about it (your action steps)?

Installed a new labor-scheduling system—a significant initiative that included the purchase of a new system from Kronos that provided labor scheduling, time and attendance, and daily/weekly/monthly dynamic budgeting.

3. What were the results? (quantify with monetary value, percentage, or numbers)

The labor scheduling initiatives yielded $5 million of annual benefit.

4. What was the strategic impact on the company?

The new labor system allowed the company to be more competitive in the marketplace with a more effective way to manage the cost of its greatest expense (labor) while simultaneously improving the ability to serve customers. The new system also provided growth capabilities:

- Allowing new standard prototype stores to open profitability
- Creating the ability to have a labor model customized for new prototypes

5. What skills and strengths did you identify in your story?

Project and team leadership. Technology know-how. Being a champion for continuous improvement and finding ways to save money for the company. Initiative in identifying and solving problems. Resource and vendor management.

The two critical stories for career success

I spoke with a client who was entering the job market after spending an extended period of time doing a mix of freelance work and raising children.

He was concerned about holes in his experience and the impact they would have on securing a good job.

He felt scared, uncomfortable, and insecure.

Another client had gone through a really tough period in

her life, which had caused her to drop some balls at work. Co-workers weren't happy, and she was concerned about how it would impact her opportunities moving forward.

She felt awkward, ashamed, and stuck.

In both these cases, there are two very important stories to tell.

The story you tell yourself

Going after new goals is challenging. The job market *is* competitive. It *isn't* easy to create art, or to get customers, or to write a book. It *is* hard to bounce back from failure or adversity. Before you start to worry about what someone else thinks about you, you have to make sure that you are thinking great things about *yourself.*

Consider the difference between these two stories.

"I have been out of the job market for five years and have not kept up on all the latest trends in technology. I am scared that prospective employers might see me as lacking. I must do whatever it takes to prove that I am worthy. I am desperate for a job. I will take any opportunity that comes my way and heave a sigh of relief, because it will mean that they accept me, despite my flaws."

How are you feeling after reading something like this? Kind of yucky and in need of a hug, right?

Consider this alternative.

"I am proud of the wide variety of experiences that I have had in my life. I can think of many times when I was put into new and challenging situations and learned quickly. Being out of the job market for a while has given me a new and refreshing perspective that makes me extremely focused and excited for new opportunities. I have enjoyed working for myself, but now I am ready to be back in a team environment where I have support and resources to get my work done. I want to work in a place that appreciates my experience. I will do a great job, and they will be lucky to have me."

That feels better, doesn't it? The first story reminds me of *Das Boot* (a film some find a classic, but what I find a most depressing German film about men stuck in a submarine) and the second story reminds me of *Rocky III*. (No one brings out "Eye of the Tiger" like Apollo Creed.)

When crafting your personal story, consider:

- What skills and strengths and ingredients am I really proud of?
- What are the threads and themes of my life experience?
- What big gifts have I received from challenges I have faced?
- What is my hero's journey?
- What is the soundtrack of my life? Is it one of the most depressing country songs of all time or an uplifting anthem?

The story you tell others

Once you get a clear and empowering story to tell yourself, you need to work on the story that will resonate and influence others. In addition to the questions you have answered for your own story, add these:

- What challenges are these (potential employers, prospective clients, resistant team members, crowd-funding prospects) facing?
- How might my background and experience help them to overcome their challenges?
- How can I clearly and powerfully respond to legitimate concerns about holes, gaps, or weaknesses in my background or skills?
- How does my total life experience give me a unique competitive advantage over fellow job applicants or business owners?
- How can I prepare to give the best interview or sales call of my life?
- How can I deliver tremendous, measurable value to the people I want to work with?

Every day, I see people with similar backgrounds and equivalent skills accomplish radically different results.

One big reason for this is the story they tell themselves and others on a daily basis.

The quality of your life is directly related to the quality of your stories.

You must craft them well.

The Persuasive Story Pattern

Nancy Duarte has spent her life studying the craft of storytelling.

As the cofounder of the world-renowned Silicon Valley presentation design firm Duarte, she has worked with some of the most influential businesspeople and thinkers in the world.

A few years ago, she was doing research for her book *Resonate*.

She studied dramatic plot structure in theater from Gustav Freytag and Aristotle's three-part story structure.

But when she studied Joseph Campbell, she got really excited.

"I got most enraptured by Joseph Campbell's Hero's Journey. It is such a beautiful pattern for transformation. You can overlay it on life, corporate change initiatives, over so many things. You can look at where you are in your life and actually plot out how your life is going to turn out."

By analyzing hundreds of the most famous speeches of all time and testing different story structures, she discovered a story pattern that mirrored the greatest speeches in the world. Her breakthrough came one morning when she overlaid both Martin Luther King Jr.'s "I Have a Dream" speech and Steve Jobs's 2007 iPhone launch speech, and they both matched her Persuasive Story Pattern.

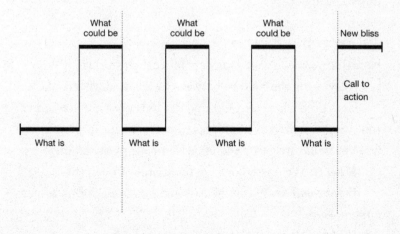

Nancy describes how to craft your story, using the Persuasive Story Pattern.

Craft the beginning

Start by describing life as the audience knows it. People should be nodding their heads in recognition because you're articulating what they already understand. This creates a bond between you and them, and opens them up to hear your ideas for change.

After you set that baseline of what is, introduce your vision of what could be. The gap between the two will throw the audience a bit off-balance, and that's a good thing—it jars them out of complacency. For instance:

What is: We fell short of our Q3 financial goals partly because we're understaffed and everyone's spread too thin.

What could be: But what if we could solve the worst of our problems by bringing in a couple of powerhouse clients? Well, we can.

Once you establish that gap, use the rest of the presentation to bridge it.

Develop the middle

Now that people in your audience realize their world is off-kilter, keep playing up the contrast between what is and what could be.

Let's go back to that Q3 update. Revenues are down, but you want to motivate employees to make up for it. Here's one way you could structure the middle of your presentation:

What is: We missed our Q3 forecast by 15 percent.

What could be: Q4 numbers must be strong for us to pay out bonuses.

What is: We have six new clients on our roster.

What could be: Two of them have the potential to bring in more revenue than our best clients do now.

What is: The new clients will require extensive retooling in manufacturing.

What could be: We'll be bringing in experts from Germany to help.

As you move back and forth between what is and what could be, the audience will find the latter more and more alluring.

Make the ending powerful

You don't want to end with a burdensome list of to-dos. Definitely include a call to action—but make it inspiring so people will want to act. Describe what I call the new bliss: how much better their world will be when they adopt your ideas.

So if you're wrapping up that Q3 update from above, you might approach it this way:

Call to action: It will take extra work from all departments to make Q4 numbers, but we can deliver products to our important new clients on time and with no errors.

New bliss: I know everyone's running on fumes—but hang in there. This is our chance to pull together like a championship team, and things will get easier if we make this work. The reward if we meet our Q4 targets? Bonuses, plus days off at the end of the year.

By defining future rewards, you show people that getting on board will be worth their effort. It'll meet their needs, not just yours.

Nancy believes that understanding story structure will not only make you a much better communicator, it will also allow you to change the world. I believe that by mastering the art of storytelling, you will be able to organize your body of work into a compelling story and present it to the world.

Your life as told by Google

Like it or not, Google is telling a story about you right now.

Go ahead, Google your name.

Hopefully you have narrated part of your story and are happy about what people have written or shared about you. If you aren't, the good news is that you can change it.

Words, images, and videos make up a multicolored tapestry of your life on the Web.

Jobs are won and business is sold by the strength of the story told by Google when people look you up on the Web. As you create your body of work, you need to package it, to illustrate it, and to tie it together in a cohesive story.

What have you done? What do people say about you? Who are you connected to? Who is connected to you and your message? What do you stand for? How does your work in Sector A tie to the project you are doing in Sector B that you are trying to sell to the Sector C?

Your body of work content map

In order to tell a cohesive story about your body of work, you need to create a content map.

When I was developing my *Escape from Cubicle Nation* blog and business, I took out a pad of paper and put a big box in the middle labeled "My People."

Then I asked myself: What do they really need?

For this business, my people were corporate employees

who wanted to quit their job and start a business. I brainstormed a bunch of different needs, then grouped them in four major categories:

• Pillar 1—Knowledge: How do you work through each stage of creating a business? What are the most efficient/effective ways to get things done? Whom can I trust?

• Pillar 2—Encouragement: Giving up a job is mighty scary. Many people are racked with self-doubt. So ongoing doses of "you are not crazy," "you go girl/guy," and "you are almost at the finish line" are very important.

• Pillar 3—Community: It is very isolating to make a big change by yourself. The more positive, supportive people surround you, the quicker you will make progress and launch your business.

• Pillar 4—Promotion. Once your business is up and running, you need exposure so your business is successful and you make enough money to quit your day job.

Once clear on what your audience needs, you can build a product/service map that follows them along a clear and defined path.

In my own coaching work, I know that people generally follow the path outlined in my book:

• They want assurance they are not crazy for leaving a good corporate job.
• They have to figure out which business to start.

- They have to figure out if there is viability in that market.
- They have to produce and test a product or service.
- They have to tell their loved ones they want to make a major career shift.
- They have to build relationships with their market, and a larger tribe of supporters, peers, and mentors.
- They have to figure out their personal financial plan.
- They have to create an implementation plan and then make it happen.
- They have to give notice at their job and leave relationships intact if things don't turn out as planned.
- They have to implement their sales and marketing plan, track their results, and make adjustments.

Develop and share the content they need

Through a period of eight years, I shared hundreds of blog posts, videos, audios, e-books, events, webinars, classes, speeches, workshops, and a book to address the particular needs of my market.

I used social media tools like my blog, Twitter, Facebook, LinkedIn, and Google+ to:

- Share knowledge (pillar 1), provide encouragement (pillar 2), and promote (pillar 4) the work of my clients and blog community.

- Create places online and in person where people in
  a similar situation could build community (pillar 3).

By consistently sharing the information that I had gathered by growing my body of work, through being self-employed, blogging, tweeting, planning, and getting through the hard times, I became well-known for this particular aspect of my body of work.

A content map for your career

If you work as an employee in a corporation or a nonprofit, your content map would still be quite similar to the one described above. Remember, organizations can build a body of work too.

Imagine all the information, resources, support, and encouragement your customers, donors, vendors, coworkers and management needs to accomplish their goals.

Share this information in meetings, presentations, e-mails, and where possible, external blogs and presentations. More and more employees of large companies are writing external blogs and building up their reputation and personal brand online.

How to create a personal content map

1. Define the specific needs of people you want to influence with your body of work. Take a piece of paper, put them in the middle, and ask yourself, "What are the major things they need to fully solve their problem?"

Sketch out the steps they need to address their problem. Think of a typical person who comes to you for help. What is the first problem they need help solving? Once that problem is solved, where do they tend to go next? Create a path of steps that ends with them realizing their goals.

2. Create content that helps them solve their problem. You have wonderful tools like blogs, podcasts, tweets, e-books and videos to create useful, valuable content that helps your people solve their problems. Couple this with more intensive support (paid teleclasses, workshops, tutorials, coaching, retreats) and they will have everything they need to solve their problem. Remember that much of your audience will solve their problem using your free material. But there will always be people who are willing to pay for more specific and individual support.

3. Sprinkle the products and services that your people really need. Think of ways to strengthen your paid offerings by adding in the specific things that will help your people succeed. As an example, the way I meet the needs of my people is to offer knowledge with blog posts, programs, workshops, and retreats. I give them inspiration with speeches, interviews with experts and cool people just like them who have made the leap successfully, daily tweets, Facebook updates, e-mails, and free calls. I give them community with live events where they can gather with like-minded people. I give them promotion by tweeting and blogging about their businesses, mentioning them in my press interviews, and making introductions with mentors and customers.

4. Organize your content map in a clear and compelling manner and promote the heck out of it. Depending on the commu-

nication style of your market, you can develop a whole range of promotional materials, including a Web-based product map, or a nicely designed set of printed materials. It is wonderful if you can get the domain name for your own name and use your-name.com as a central place to host all of your content.

With a clear content map and plan, you are ready to focus on the quality of your content.

How to communicate clearly

"Let the wild rumpus start."

The first time I read this passage to my three-year old from the classic Maurice Sendak book *Where the Wild Things Are*, I felt a wave of pleasure and a flashback to my own childhood. I had forgotten how ripe and tantalizing the words were; perfectly chosen, crisp, simple, and powerful.

Why isn't all writing like that?

As readers, we hunger for clear, useful, insightful, and inspiring words.

As writers, we long to speak the truth and say something relevant and important.

But somehow in our professional lives, we are taught to convolute, complicate, and butcher perfectly good language when communicating with users, clients, customers, employees, and partners.

How can we clean up our stories so that we evoke the spirit of a well-written book? Here are some places to demonstrate clear and effective language.

In presentations: Trust your instincts

In my prior days as a management consultant, I was brought into a project at a large multinational company with short notice and no information. For four hours, I sat in a dark conference room with a bunch of serious-looking executives and listened to an "overview" presentation that was a minimum of three hundred PowerPoint slides, with eye-crossing graphs, charts, and bullets. At the end of the presentation, although I wouldn't admit it to anyone in public, I still had no idea what the project was about. Seriously. None whatsoever. And I was no green bean; I had participated in large projects in large organizations for many years. Finally, once I was able to corner a smart-looking person, I said, "Can you tell me in ten words or less what this project is about?"

"Sure," he said. "It is a reorganization."

They could have saved 299 slides and four hours' worth of my billable time if they had just said those four words.

There is a conspiracy cooked up by marketing wonks, consultants, and executives to pay for words by the pound, and to question the intelligence of a corporate "professional" who does not create complex and obtuse presentations. They are wrong. Your instinct to keep things clean and simple is right. A few tips:

• Use clear language. As much as you may feel pressure to use the fancy words in your industry, stick with clear, descriptive language. Avoid jargon, clichés, and insider metaphors. If your audience is highly technical, use the terms that they relate to and expect. If it is a mixed crowd, give a variety of clear, topic-appropriate examples, with a few specific technical references that relate to that portion of your audience.

- Focus your topic. Know what your primary message is, and support it with no more than three sub-points. Cramming every feature, benefit, angle, or alternative into a presentation will just overwhelm and confuse your audience. If they want more information, they will ask for it, and then you can get to the real purpose of your presentation, which is dialogue and interaction.

- Take the Presentation Zen approach to mixing words and graphics. Designer and author Garr Reynolds, founder of the *Presentation Zen* blog and a series of bestselling books of the same name, suggests that you use powerful graphic images to anchor ideas in the minds of your audience. Cut most of the words out of your slides. If you have to say "I know you can't see the details of this chart, but . . . ," you shouldn't include it. Choose your graphics carefully, and make sure they truly help illustrate a point.

In blogs: Speak your truth

Blogs are a fantastic vehicle for sharing your story and showcasing your body of work. Blog culture encourages open, personal, and straight communication. But we still fall victim to being either too boring and generic, or too self-indulgent with "Here are twelve more pictures of my cat and kids plus a personal rant" posts. Instead:

Write for your audience

Some bloggers write about whatever strikes their fancy, and it suits them well. I tend to stick close to my readers. Questions that guide my content include:

- What problems do they face?
- What really scares them?
- What is not being said on this subject on other news sources or blogs?
- What can I share that will make their life easier?
- How can I make them feel more supported and confident?
- Who can I put them in contact with (via links or references) that will give them good information and advice?
- What will be fun and interesting to write about?

Use your own voice

Your head can play tricks on you when choosing topics. Mostly, it will play on your fears and insecurities of needing to appear "smart" or "hip." Dig deeper and write what you feel is the truth. Your truth will be different than anyone else's, so many are bound to disagree, but that is part of the fun. If you worry about how smart or important you sound, your writing will come out stilted and insincere. A passage from the delightful book *If You Want to Write* by Brenda Ueland sums it up nicely:

> [I]nspiration does not come like a bolt, nor is it kinetic, energetic striving, but it comes to us slowly and quietly and all the time, though we must regularly and every day give it a chance to start flowing, and prime it with a little solitude and idleness. I learned that when writing you should feel not like Lord Byron on a mountaintop but like a child stringing beads in

kindergarten—happy, absorbed, and quietly putting one bead in front of another.

Use your superpowers for good

This is a favorite saying of my friend Marilyn Scott-Waters, a talented illustrator who has given away more than 3 million lovingly illustrated paper toys on her website thetoymaker .com. Snark and gossip are part of our lives and can be entertaining in a superficial kind of way. But if you are going to spend hours and hours researching and writing and opining, why not do it for the purpose of uplifting and enlightening? There are enough forces in the world right now bent on humiliation, death, and destruction. So voice your honest thoughts, just do so without shaming, scaring, or ridiculing the subjects of your opinions.

In sales copy: Cut the hype

Most of us have to sell our ideas in writing. If you work for yourself and sell a product or service, you may have to create marketing materials or a sales letter. There are well-documented copywriting recipes that specify what color or font size to make your headlines, which "words that sell" to use at which part of the letter, and how to format and use testimonials from satisfied customers. Study these examples, as you are bound to learn something from them, but don't become a slave to a formula. In addition:

• Show your personality. Don't suddenly change your voice just because you are writing a sales letter. Use the style and language that you know makes your audience comfortable.

Don't be afraid to be playful and funny, or serious and straight-forward, if it fits within the style and spirit of what you are selling.

• Don't insult your audience with infomercial nonsense like "But wait, there's more!" We are all tired of reading advertising copy that jumps out and screams at us. And as Seth Godin says, "The most effective technique is making stuff worth talking about in the first place. True viral marketing happens not when the marketer plans for it or targets bloggers or skate-boarders or pirates with goatees, but when the item/service/event is worth talking about."

• Use the "slime gauge." Put yourself in the place of a poten-tial customer. Read your words and see how you feel. Do you have a vague sense of embarrassment? Do you have a sudden urge to take a shower? Go back and scrub your document of any marketing slime and focus on the real, tangible benefits that make you truly proud of your product or service.

In messages to potential partners, customers, or mentors: Bring back foreplay

E-mail is a great way to begin to build a relationship with some-one who interests you. But too often, we forget all rules of human interaction and jump right to a jarring, intimate request, such as:

"I see that your blog reaches a similar target audience as mine. I am sure they would be interested in my product, so could you link to it? I will link to you if you link to me."

Such crude, direct language turns me off immediately. In-stead:

• Treat online relationships like all relationships. Just as you wouldn't go up to someone you had never met at a networking event and kiss them on the lips, you shouldn't demand something the first time you approach someone online. "Link exchange" is a thing of the past. Before someone knows if they want to share you and your ideas with their audience, they want to get to know and trust you. So let that intimacy and trust build naturally, based on mutual interest and exchange of ideas. If a joint venture, book review, link exchange, or product endorsement is meant to happen, it will. And you may just make a real advocate and friend in the process.

• Focus each part of the e-mail conversation in the moment, not on your "closing goal." In personal and business settings, you can feel when someone is going through the motions to try to "close a deal" with you. The most obvious examples are an overzealous suitor in a bar, or an enthusiastic relative recently introduced to a business scheme who is hot to sell you new skin products. Avoid this uncomfortable dynamic by just enjoying each e-mail interaction as you have it. Look for ways that you can support, inform, and encourage your "object of affection." If there is not a natural momentum or energy, back off and put your attention elsewhere.

• Be respectful of the other's time. You may find that you build a natural, friendly connection with someone that you really admire. Or you may develop a truly supportive and friendly mailing list of interested customers. Do not jeopardize this relationship by asking for too much input, or sending too many messages. E-mail clutter is a real problem these days, and if you go overboard, you will soon reinforce a connection between your name and the delete button.

Common sense is rarely common practice. So if some of this advice gets you ostracized, ridiculed, or even fired, all I can say is "Welcome to the other side." Your audience will thank you for standing up for truth and clarity.

Let the wild rumpus start.

A great story needs great drama

One time when my dad and Diane visited us in Arizona, we all stayed at Saguaro Lake Ranch, a local bed-and-breakfast in the Tonto National Forest in Mesa. While I was inside the lodge writing, my five-year old daughter Angela Rose lost a tooth.

She came to find me, and told me the story of how it fell out.

She then dictated a letter to me for the tooth fairy. Here it is exactly as she told it to me.

Dear Tooth Fairy:

I lost a tooth.
I had bacon.
I felt my tooth, it was a little bit loose.
I went swimming.
And then I ate a cracker.
And then I thought there was a nut in it.
And then I felt my tooth and it was out.
And then I went to the hotel.

And then I knocked on the door four times.

And then I showed my Mom.

And then she's like OH. MY. GOD.

> From,
>
> Angela

She retold this story to every person who noticed that her bottom tooth was missing, including my local Starbucks coffee crew, neighbors, her teachers, and the school principal.

Each time, she would end with the dramatic OH. MY. GOD.

Did you really need to know about the bacon and swimming, or how she ate a cracker that ended up containing her tooth? Probably not. But it makes the story much more entertaining.

Another noteworthy story that went viral on the Internet was creative director Ryan Kutscher's Craigslist ad for his bike, which illustrates how, for Ryan's ideal customer, colorful language was a key part of adding humor and drama to the story.

```
Grab a paper bag, breathe into it, and
calm your ass down. You're hyperventilat-
ing because you ain't never seen a deal
like this before. Now collect yourself,
then keep reading this incredible de-
scription that barely serves to do jus-
tice to my 2010 Felt Gridlock [sic] 3-speed
fixed-gear bike. Yes, 3-SPEED FIXED-GEAR.
Also known as the greatest bike the city
```

has ever had the privilege of existing around.

What makes this bike so much better than every other bike that has ever been pedaled? Glad you asked. It starts with the paint scheme. It looks like Iron Man if Iron Man were a bike. That's bold, son. Curb appeal. It's probably also why some piece of trash stole the front tire that originally came with this beauty. Why didn't he steal the whole bike? Because he knew he wasn't man enough. That's OK, I replaced it with something that looks even more boss. The next thing is the genuine leather seat. My taint has had a love/hate relationship with this particular bit of the machine. But it's got those swanky brass rivets, so I can't stay mad that it smashed my prostate and has likely rendered fatherhood impossible. But let's face it, I'd rather have had a bike than a kid.

Details, humor, and context can bring your stories to life and connect with the emotions of your audience.

How to establish credibility with your story

We have all squirmed through this scenario:

You sign up for a conference and get really excited about

learning critical things to grow your career or business. You invest time, money, and energy to clear your agenda so you can be there.

The lights dim and the first speaker is introduced. They look friendly and pleasant, and start the talk off on a good foot. They mention that they grew up in Omaha, Nebraska, and got an academic scholarship to Yale. Then they were president of their fraternity and maintained a 4.0 grade point average while starting a highly successful business in their dorm room.

Five minutes in, you are starting to want to stab yourself in the eye with a pencil if it would mean helping them get to the point of the presentation.

Ten minutes in, they are still sharing the fine points of their illustrious career, awards they have won, and famous people who beg and plead for their advice. "And then the pope said to me, 'Jim, I am really in a quandary here. . . .'"

Fifteen minutes in, you are wanting to poke *their* eye out with a pencil, even if it means serving a short jail sentence. Anything to stop their incessant bragging.

"If I were them," you scream to yourself, "I would stop blowing smoke and get to the point of the presentation, which is about me and my needs."

Right?

Well, almost right.

There is a fine line between establishing necessary credibility with a new audience and being a complete egomaniac.

What your audience needs to know in order to trust what you say

Never assume that people in a new audience know anything about you. I spoke at a wonderful local event in my hometown of Mesa, Arizona, and besides my friend Clate Mask, CEO of Infusionsoft, and my former client and ace photographer Ivan Martinez, no one knew who I was. I got to know my bright and talented fellow presenter in the session itself, so we didn't have any context or background about each other to plan the session. So when I did my introduction, even though I was speaking to my own community, I had to establish my background so that they knew enough about me to trust my advice.

A new audience needs to know:

Your formal education or training that prepares you to do your work

If you have a degree from Harvard, or a PhD in engineering from MIT, tell them. Rather than bragging, this puts their mind at ease. If you are talking to a group that values community education, tell them. When Clate did the keynote at Mesa Community College about how he grew his company from a ramen-noodle-eating group of three broke guys with big dreams into a $30 million company with two hundred employees (now approaching seven hundred), what did he mention about his education? That he started it at Mesa Community College. This was extremely meaningful to newer entrepreneurs and students in the audience.

Key parts of your own life story to prove you did what you teach

Are you teaching lawyers how to set up a virtual law practice like my client Rachel Rodgers did? Tell them how you did it yourself and what you learned from the experience. Are you proud of the fact that you grew a great company while raising your kids as a single parent? If that would establish credibility with your audience, tell that part of the story.

Specific examples of how you have helped other people just like them get great results

• Numbers of clients ("I have worked with over 350 small- and medium-size businesses." "Every one of the 250 high school seniors we had in our program went on to a college or university."). Concrete numbers mean something.

• Business results of the clients you worked with, even if you haven't worked with many ("Three of my clients went from zero to $30,000 in revenue in their side hustle in the year after working with me."). I like to tell my friend Ramit Sethi that he is a possessed madman when it comes to tracking concrete re- sults from his clients, but that is only to keep his ego in check. He is *masterful* at it and constantly reminds us of the concrete results readers of his blog and participants in his programs have gotten from following his advice.

Street credibility
As much as social media pundits like to exclaim "old media is dead," there is still huge street credibility in mainstream press mentions. Mention:

- Mainstream press ("Featured in the *New York Times*." "Named one of the Top 25 Entrepreneurs to Follow by the *Wall Street Journal*.")
- Awards and honors ("Best Business Book of 2011." "Top 100 Women on Twitter." "Voted Most Likely to Succeed in high school.")
- Influential people's view of you (Called "one of the

best presentation designers I have ever seen" by
Nancy Duarte.)

Do you need to say *all* this in your introduction?

Of course not. That would make you a blowhard. But you do
need to review all of the concrete things you could share about
yourself and choose the specific information that:

- Is most relevant to that audience. (If you are
  speaking at Harvard, mention your degree. If you
  are speaking at a start-up conference, mention
  your personal bootstrapping story.)

- Will shut down the nagging doubt in the audience's mind.

  "Is she too young to talk about this topic?" "Does
  this consultant have any real-world experience
  building a software product?" "Is she one of
  those people who just teaches others to make
  money on the Internet so that she can make
  money off those people on the Internet?" One
  time, a local friend who I had known for a few
  years said to me, "You know what my problem
  is with you? You are like one of those people
  who create an infomercial to teach people how
  to create infomercials." To which I responded,
  a bit stunned, "Do you have any idea what I
  do, and have you ever read my book?" It turned

out that he didn't, and he hadn't. I thanked him immensely for the feedback, because if he was brave enough to say it to my face, it meant that there were a whole bunch more people who thought it and just said it behind my back.

- Will set the stage for people to comfortably trust that the advice you will give them in your presentation is sound and tested.

  Your audience will think, "OK, phew, she has successfully started a company, raised venture capital, sold the company, and started and sold four others. I can trust what she tells me."

I was taught by my parents and grandparents to be humble, to be in service of others, and to always put others' needs above my own. This is a fantastic heritage, and I am so thankful for the teaching, since I think it helps me be a respectful and decent human being.

However, in business situations, sometimes in order to gain the trust of the audience so you can be of service, you must tell a compelling story that establishes credibility and showcases your body of work.

Finding the thread that ties your story together

In this chapter, we have examined:

- the two stories you must have in alignment to influence your audience—the story you tell yourself and the story you tell others.

- the craft of storytelling, and the Persuasive Story Pattern that Nancy Duarte recommends for maximum impact and results.

- how to create a content map to guide the information and projects you share that addresses the specific needs of your audience so that when people search for you online, they find rich examples of your body of work.

- the importance of clear and compelling language in all of your communication.

- how to establish credibility by highlighting the ingredients that are relevant and impressive to each audience you speak to.

The final step in creating a clear and compelling story about your body of work is to find a thread of connection with your audience as you craft specific messages for different situations.

1. The high-level story

Your high-level story is the summary of your body of work that you most often find in "Bios" and "About" pages on websites. A story at this level is crafted around:

- What are the themes that weave through your work? Look at all the work you have done in your life and see if you notice overarching themes. You might find "pursuit of excellence," "scientific experimentation," or "fascination with other cultures." When I did this exercise, I found that most of the work I have done falls into the categories of "freedom," "transformation," and "learning."

- What are your roots, and how do you want them reflected in your story?
- What are the ingredients you want to highlight in your story? In some cases, you may choose to only list your professional skills and experience, while in others, you may include personal information like hobbies, interests, and family status
- What is the right amount of credibility to sprinkle in your story? In this kind of story, you might want to mention a few of your educational accomplishments, accolades, or awards. Use enough to let people know that you are competent but not so much that they get distracted from the bigger message of your body of work.

2. The interview or client story

When you are applying for a job or speaking to a perspective client, you want to craft your story according to specific parameters. For this story, review:

- What are the specific needs of your audience (review your content map)?
- Which of your roots, ingredients, and experience will make them feel confident and comfortable about your ability to meet their needs?
- Which stories will best illustrate your roots, ingredients, and experience?
- What specific answers do you have for any perceived gaps or weak areas?

3. The networking story

When you bump into a new person at the gym, or attend a business networking event for the first time, you don't want to launch into a lengthy list of your ingredients. Choose a short phrase that will help them understand what you do, while helping spark a good discussion:

- "I am a lawyer who is obsessed with lean business principles."
- "I work with people who feel stuck in their business or career."
- "I am a nurse with a passion for Italian cooking."
- "I am a former Olympic athlete, and my new interests are philanthropy and fashion."

The most important thing to remember about the skill of storytelling in the new world of work is that you must *customize your message to the audience you are speaking to*. Because you will have an ever-expanding set of work modes, ingredients, and experiences, you don't need to overwhelm your audience with a laundry list of everything you have ever done.

Your ability to tell compelling, truthful, engaging stories will decide the lasting impact your body of work has on the world.

Tell them well.

CONCLUSION

When I first set out to write this book, I was excited to share a new framework that I had seen emerge from the coaching work I had done with hundreds of clients over more than two decades.

My goal was to find a set of "new" skills for the world of work in the twenty-first century that would provide options, flexibility, and freedom to workers across every work mode, in every industry.

When I initially thought of including some of my dad's story in the first chapter, I was excited to hear his perspective on the two decades he had spent restoring the Port Costa School. It seemed like the perfect metaphor.

During our interview about the school, my dad told me that when he was living in San Anselmo in 1967, someone wrote a letter to the editor of the local paper, complaining about the decaying downtown storefronts.

"This really bothered me," he said. "I wanted to do something about it."

Since he was a photographer, he took pictures of every storefront along the main downtown strip on San Anselmo Avenue. Then he called seven of his friends who were skilled architects and designers. He passed out a couple of photographs to each of them and asked if they would be willing to draw a picture of what they would do to improve the storefronts, as well as what they could do to an ugly concrete parking lot that backed up to a creek that ran parallel to the downtown. All of them agreed and set to work with the new designs.

When the drawings were all done, he took pictures of each of them. Then he created a slide slow that included pictures of the decaying storefronts, along with the "new, improved" drawings. He set up community meetings in a couple of different locations in town and invited the residents of San Anselmo to attend. Many of them did.

"When they saw the new drawings, they started applauding!" my dad said. "They got really excited about the possibilities."

He did the show for the downtown merchants, and they were amazed by what they saw. The merchants and city government mobilized, and over the course of a decade, the downtown was slowly upgraded. A beautiful new park was designed to replace the ugly concrete parking lot by the creek based on the drawing by my dad's friend Dan Goltz. It was renamed Creek Park.

In this small project in San Anselmo, in 1967, my dad utilized every one of the skills I include in the Body of Work Success Framework.

He connected to his roots. He had a deeply instilled sense of community pride and service, reaching back to the way his father raised him on the farm in Yuba City. "Our farm was immaculate," he said. "From the time I can remember, my dad had us pick up trash along the road and clean every spot of the farm."

He relied on his ingredients. He depended on his photography skills and experience from his role at Pacific Gas and Electric, where he used to run community meetings up and down the state of California.

He chose the work mode of volunteer. Instead of waiting to get in a position of influence or authority, he chose to do this project as a concerned member of the community, since he thought that from that perspective, he could garner more trust (in later years, he did join the city council and eventually become mayor).

He overcame his fear and hesitation. Since he was neither an elected official nor local merchant, he had to face his fears head on in order to do something about the decaying downtown.

He created a project to address the problem. He designed community meetings where he could show people concrete examples of the area's potential.

He gathered a team of collaborators. He reached out to talented peer mentors who had the exact skills he needed to complete his project.

He defined a big part of personal success as having a positive impact on the community. Even though he didn't earn a dime with the project, he felt tremendous satisfaction when he saw the results.

He told a compelling story. He moved through Nancy Duarte's presentation framework from "what is" (the decaying storefronts) to what "could be" (the drawings of the reimagined storefronts), and he inspired his audience to action.

I got chills as I heard my dad tell this story. I suddenly realized that I had watched him use these skills in his life and career for years, but it wasn't until I wrote this book that I truly understood the underlying framework, since I was used to looking at his career, volunteer work, and personal life through separate lenses.

The one thing I knew all along? That he was a very fulfilled and happy person who navigated a life of challenge and uncertainty with grit and success.

I hope that the stories I shared in this book of the creative and brave people like Amanda Wang, David Batstone, Mike Carson, Rafe Eric Biggs, Kyle Durand, John Legend, and Desiree Adaway will inspire you to take some risks of your own, with the purpose of feeling more alive, engaged, connected, and excited in your work.

Viewing your career as a body of work will give you more choice, financial security, and creative freedom. The world is not going to serve up neat career tracks anymore. You cannot guarantee that your business or nonprofit will survive in a constantly changing economic landscape. But you can choose the kinds of projects that are worth completing and the type of life that is worth living.

This book is part of my own body of work, and it is just beginning. Join me at pamelaslim.com/bodyofwork to learn more about the people profiled in the book, to access additional tools and resources, and to share questions, thoughts, images, and videos of *your* body of work.

My wish for you is that you create a full-color, full-contact life that brings great value to the world and great joy and success to you and your family.

Let the creating begin.

ACKNOWLEDGMENTS

This book, like my first, was a true team effort. Sheila Sanders, thank you for being an amazing partner. Your patience, care, and professionalism allowed me the space to write when I needed to write. To Steve, Cheyn, Mathias, and Kavin, thank you for being generous enough to share your wife and mom with me. To my dear friend and marketing partner Tim Grahl, I appreciate both the person that you are and the care with which you do your work. To your team at Out:think, Joseph Hinton and Lauren Baker, thanks for keeping my business running and making us all look good. To Kyle Durand and Cynthia Durand, your love for business systems is only outmatched by your kindness. Thank you for your expert guidance and fierce friendship.

To Jill Murphy, Andre Blackman, Abe Cajudo, Willie Jackson, Ericka Hines, and Mike Ambassador Bruny, thank you for our wonderful e-mail chains and shared laments and celebrations. I am proud and honored to be your friend.

To my collaborative partners and peer mentors Jonathan

Fields, Ramit Sethi, Michele Woodward, and Chris Guille-beau, thank you for always challenging my thinking and push-ing me to excel in life and business. To Charlie Gilkey and Angela Wheeler, thank you for your powerful friendship and amazing coaching. I am so proud of the body of work we created together in our Lift Off community. To my partner in prose, Betsy Rapoport, your mastery of the craft of writing is inspira-tional. To my favorite Canadian, Michael Bungay-Stanier, thank you for stepping in to support me and this book right when I needed it. I will never forget your personal care and expert coaching. This book would not have gotten written without you.

To Dan Pink and Nancy Duarte, thank you for giving feedback on the early ideas for this book and providing support and encouragement. You are both my heroes, and I can only hope that my body of work has the impact and reach that yours has had in the world.

To Seth Godin, Guy Kawasaki and Martha Beck, thank you for being my steady council of wise advice, support, and encouragement.

To the 350 members of the Body of Work Advisory Board, I appreciate your willingness to receive random e-mails from me about a whole range of unrelated topics. You input and in-sight were so valuable!

To my clients, you are the soul and heartbeat of this book. Our intense, inspiring, sometimes tough and emotional con-versations pushed me to want to create something that will allow you to continually grow and develop, through your busi-nesses and beyond them. Thank you for trusting me with your confidence, and for investing in me and my family.

To my agent, Joelle Delbourgo, thank you for not only believing in me but for being passionate about this book. You inspired me to make it happen. To my kind, talented, and patient editor, Emily Angell, thank you for providing just the right blend of encouragement and firm nudges. To Adrian Zackheim, Will Weiser, Margot Stamas, and the entire Portfolio team, thank you for believing in this book. To Emily Rapoport, who edited my first book, thank you for taking this book proposal to heart. I will never forget that you were the one who found me among a sea of business bloggers and started my professional writing career.

To my best friend, Desiree Adaway, thank you for always being there for everything.

To Master Fiori, thank you for your expert instruction, guidance, and friendship. I am so proud to be your black belt student. To my martial arts family, thank you for pushing me to grow mentally, physically, and spiritually.

To my family, thank you for your never-ending support and encouragement. I am so proud to be related to you!

To the Singers and the Dardens, thank you for your kinship and prayers. Our family is strong because your families are strong. *Ahéhee'*.

To my neighbors, who always look out for my family and make our community a beautiful and safe place to live. I love you all.

Finally, I want to say a special extra thank you to Abe Cajudo for reminding me on a daily basis of my deepest root—that everyone on earth has gifts and talents that are meant to be heard, no matter how long it may take the world to hear them. I believe in your mission, your heart, and your work. Keep fighting.

NOTES AND SELECTED FURTHER READING

Throughout this book, several resources are cited. Below is a collection of references and recommended resources for further reading. All resources listed below can also be found at www.pamelaslim.com/bodyofwork.

Chapter 1

7   **The secret to high performance:** Pink, Daniel H. *Drive: The Surprising Truth About What Motivates Us.* (New York: Riverhead Books, 2011), 207–8.

Chapter 2

17   **It was seven thirty:** Additional information on Amanda Wang and her personal mission can be found at http://thefightwithinus .com.

26   **Victor Frankl, in his stark and powerful new book:** Frankl, Viktor E. *Man's Search for Meaning.* (Boston: Beacon Press, 2006), 109.

Chapter 3

35 As David recounted in hs book: Additional information on Not
For Sale can be found at http://www.notforsalecampaign.org.

43 Canadian entrepreneur Dan Martell: See Dan Martell's website:
clarity.fm.

44 Brené Brown is a shame and vulnerability researcher: Brown,
Brené. *Daring Greatly: How the Courage to Be Vulnerable Transforms
the Way We Live, Love, Parent, and Lead.* (New York: Gotham,
2012), 61.

46 Charlie Gilkey is a writer: Additional information on Charlie
Gilkey and his website can be found at www.productiveflourishing
.com.

Chapter 4

55 In a study conducted: A link to the study conducted by Intuit and
cited by the NextSpace CEO can be found at http://qz.com/65279
/40-of-americas-workforce-will-be-freelancers-by-2020.

57 The rise of advertising: The quote about Jenna Marbles' online
business is from the *New York Times*: www.nytimes.com/2013/04/
14/fashion/jenna-marbles.html?pagewanted=all&_r=0.

58 Thanks to Emilie Wapnick: Emilie Wapnick's website is located
at http://puttylike.com.

Chapter 5

77 Now their hip-hop blog: Mike B. and Mike C.'s hip-hop blog,
Illroots, can be found at http://illroots.com.

79 As Scott Belsky, the author: Learn more about Scott Belsky's
Behance and 99U at http://99u.com.

89 **Few people are as enthusiastic:** Ramit Sethi's blog post can be found at: www.iwillteachyoutoberich.com/blog/wednesday-workout -testing-your-assumptions.

89 **Brian Clark of Copyblogger:** Brian Clark of Copyblogger has built a thriving business. Learn more about him at www.copyblogger .com/author/Brian.

90 **the *Business Model Generation* handbook:** *Business Model Generation* is a handbook for visionaries, game changers, and challengers striving to defy outmoded business models and design tomorrow's enterprises.

99 **in order to keep America great:** Watch Piers Morgan interview LL Cool J on CNN at www.cnn.com/video/?/video/bestoftv/2012 /02/10/pmt-ll-cool-j.cnn&iref=videosearch and at www.cnn.com/ video/?/video/bestoftv/2012/02/10/pmt-ll-cool-j.cnn&iref=video search.

Chapter 6

103 **I was integrating the work:** Learn more about Rafe Eric Biggs and his personal journey at www.somaevolution.org.

107 **There are many ways to run:** For more of Richard Branson's insight into how to build a business: Branson, Richard. *Business Stripped Bare: Adventures of a Global Entrepreneur.* (New York: Portfolio/Penguin, 2011), 6.

110 **One of the deepest layers:** Beck, Martha. *Steering by Starlight: The Science and Magic of Finding Your Destiny.* (New York: Rodale Books, 2009, Kindle Edition), 655–63.

123 **The answer is simple:** Get more wisdom from Anne Lamott on her personal Facebook page: https://www.facebook.com/AnneLamott /posts/317015661761417.

Chapter 7

129 Kyle Durand accomplished a lot: Learn more about Kyle Durand at http://kyledurand.com.

141 Gladwell describes these types: Gladwell, Malcolm. *The Tipping Point.* (New York: Little, Brown and Company, 2000), 30.

148 Seth Godin said something: Read Seth Godin's blog posts at: http://sethgodin.typepad.com/seths_blog/2010/11/no-knight-no -shining-armor.html.

Chapter 8

160 After being a supportig player: For more on John Legend, see: www.escapefromcubiclenation.com/2010/12/02/if-john-legend -were-still-best-known-for-being-an-excel-cowboy/ and www .oprahs-next-chapter/Oprahs-Next-Chapter-John-Legend.

162 career coach Marty Nemko: Learn more about Marty Nemko and his perspective on what it takes to be a winner on BusinessInsider. com: www.businessinsider.com/real-winners-dont-have-work-life -balance-2013-5.

163 In her bestselling book: Sandberg, Sheryl. *Lean In: Women, Work, and the Will to Lead.* (New York: Knopf, 2013).

170 Brené Brown was featured: Watch Oprah interview Brené Brown at www.oprah.com/own-super-soul-sunday/Oprah-and-Brene -Brown.

178 Over the years, I have: Find more of Henri J.M. Nouwen's inspiring quotes at www.goodreads.com/author/quotes/4837.Henri_ J_M_Nouwen.

Chapter 9

201 **Designer and author Garr Reynolds:** Find out more about Garr Reynolds and Presentation Zen at: www.presentationzen.com.

202 **Brenda Ueland sums it up:** Ueland, Brenda. *If You Want to Write: A Book About Art, Independence and Spirit.* (BN Publishing, 2010).

204 **as Seth Godin says:** Seth Godin's quote from "In sales copy: Cut the hype" can be found on his blog at http://sethgodin.typepad .com/seths_blog/2007/09/yet-another-fro.html.

207 **Grab a paper bag:** Ryan Kutscher's hilarious Craigslist ad can be found here: http://mashable.com/2013/05/07/craigslist-ad-bike.

INDEX